Women
Killers

© Haynes Publishing, 2014

The right of Claire Welch to be identified as the author of this Work has been asserted
by her in accordance with the Copyright, Designs & Patents Act 1988.

All rights reserved. No part of this publication may be reproduced, stored in a
retrieval system or transmitted, in any form or by any means, electronic, mechanical,
photocopying, recording or otherwise, without prior permission in writing from
the publisher.

First published in 2014

A catalogue record for this book is available from the British Library

ISBN: 978-0-85733-667-5

Published by Haynes Publishing, Sparkford, Yeovil,
Somerset BA22 7JJ, UK
Tel: 01963 442030 Fax: 01963 440001
Int. tel: +44 1963 442030 Int. fax: +44 1963 440001
E-mail: sales@haynes.co.uk
Website: www.haynes.co.uk

Haynes North America Inc., 861 Lawrence Drive, Newbury Park, California 91320, USA

Images © Mirrorpix

Creative Director: Kevin Gardner
Designed for Haynes by BrainWave

Printed and bound in the US

Women
Killers

From The Case Files of
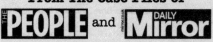

Claire Welch

Contents

Introduction

Murder is a terrifying factor of life, but when the perpetrator is a woman it somehow makes it much more difficult for most of society to comprehend. In truth, women killers have been a real fact of life throughout history.

Mary Ansell poisoned her own sister in the late 19th century in order to collect life insurance, and became the youngest woman, at the age of 22, to be hanged in the "modern era". There was a great deal of public pressure for a reprieve on the grounds of her gender and age, but her act was deemed premeditated and the execution went ahead. Ruth Ellis was the last woman to be executed in Britain when she was convicted for the murder of her lover, David Blakely, in 1955.

Less than 10 years later, Myra Hindley was identified as one of the notorious Moors murderers, alongside Ian Brady. The couple were found responsible for the deaths of five children. Aileen Wuornos, who became a gymslip hooker at the age of 11, went on a killing spree in 1989 and murdered seven men in the United States in less than 12 months. Her murderous attacks were deemed to be revenge for the hardships she'd endured throughout her own life. Beverley Allitt was convicted in 1993 of murdering four children, attempting to murder three others and causing grievous bodily harm to a further six children while working as a nurse at Grantham District (now Grantham and Kesteven) Hospital in Lincolnshire. Meanwhile, Rosemary "Rose" West was yet to be discovered. In 1995, she was convicted of the torture and murder of at least 10 young women alongside her husband, Fred West, at the couple's home in Gloucester.

One of the first women to become notorious in history and folklore for murder was Countess Elizabeth Bathory, who was widowed at the age of 44 in 1604. She returned to her powerful Hungarian estates, after a time at the family castle in Vienna, so that her torture sessions could be carried out in private. Bathory came from an extremely wealthy and religiously influential family, born in 1560 at a time when there were numerous battles between the Austrian Hapsburgs and Ottoman Empire. She grew up on an estate in Transylvania, where her cousin Stephen was prince, and planned to unite Europe against the Turks. Prince Stephen was also a savage man, and, say historians, well known for his deranged behaviour. This is often cited with regard to Barthory's own mental instability, and as proof that the family was plagued by mental illness. Bathory's childhood was extremely difficult, despite her privileged upbringing, due to a brain disorder associated with increased aggression. She possibly also suffered from epilepsy, and was definitely subject to fits and would often fly into uncontrolled rages.

In the 16th and 17th centuries, it wasn't uncommon among aristocrats to treat servants with disdain and contempt. Brutal beatings were commonplace, and death not unknown at a time when a servant was deemed a lesser human being. There was no accountability for the ruling classes – peasants had to endure whatever their lords and masters meted out. Bathory enjoyed the power she had inherited on her marriage, which, coupled with a vicious impulsiveness, led to some of the most horrendous murders of all time – which still remain firmly entrenched in folklore. Anna Darvulia was a woman said to have encouraged the atrocious behaviour of Bathory. On Darvulia's death, the countess was joined in her evil pursuits by Erzsi Majorova, alongside others, who encouraged and enjoyed the barbaric torture of young women and girls who were either lured, or kidnapped, for the purpose.

By 1609, pretty young women and girls had begun to disappear from nearby villages, while daughters of lesser nobility, sent to the Hungarian estates for tutoring, were never seen again. Local families were faced with a terrible dilemma. To speak out would mean extreme punishment; apart from talking of their fears to local priests there was nothing they could do. After her husband's death, Bathory refined her torture methods and continued her atrocities unabated. Many of the girls were beaten, often by Bathory herself, until their bodies were badly swollen – the favoured form of torture – while others were burned and then dismembered. Some of the girls had their mouths sewn shut, or were forced to eat strips of their own flesh. Genitals were burned and mutilated, and a large number of the young women had needles stuck into their already battered bodies. Eventually, the torture came to an end. Trials were held and there were executions in 1610. One servant girl who refused to testify against the countess – the only one – had her eyes gouged out and her breasts cut off before she was burned at the stake. Three defendants were executed. Two had their fingers removed by hot pinchers before they were burned at the stake. Another was beheaded, while a fourth defendant was sentenced to life imprisonment after testimony showed that she had been bullied, using extreme measures, into taking part. Bathory didn't attend a trial, but was imprisoned in a bricked-up room by her family, fed only through "slots", and died in incarceration four years later. After her death there were rumours that she had had young girls butchered in order to bathe in their blood, in search of eternal youth, although there are no court records that support this claim. Bathory was an extremely rare female killer, known to indulge in vampire and cannibal rituals, and it was more likely that she was sexually excited by the sight of blood – using it in dedicated "ceremonies" – than obsessed with youthfulness.

Despite the heinous crimes of Bathory, to this day criminologists agree – and it's one of the few issues on which they do agree – that men are much more likely to commit murder than women. But are the gender barriers changing when it comes to murder? In the 21st century there is more equality for women, but it's still a fact that society is extremely perturbed by female killers. Today people the world over are far more accepting of the changes that have occurred during the past 100 years. It's not uncommon for girls and boys to play the same sports at school. Girls' football and cricket are now widely accepted, and boys are playing hockey in primary schools – once a girls' only sport, unless played by boys at public school – as well as rounders. It's not frowned on for a man to become a house husband these days, and women are claiming more top jobs and equal pay alongside their male counterparts, according to some reports. In Britain, in 2013, it was announced that women are the main breadwinners in 41 per cent of households, and, on average, earn up to £14,000 more each year than their partners or husbands. So the tables are slowly being turned. Or are they? Speaking in September 2013, Frances O'Grady, the first TUC Secretary General, argued that women are facing increasing discrimination. She told the TUC conference that she challenged the notion that conditions for working women were improving. Ms O'Grady said: "Women tend to get stuck in jobs and industries which are vulnerable, and pregnant women are facing growing discrimination. In a recession, bad bosses find it easier to sack people and it's women who go to the front of the queue." In the autumn of 2013, TUC analysis showed there were nearly 5 million people in the UK who were jobless (which was double the official figures) and that women were bearing the brunt. In any case, whether women are climbing further up the ladder, financially, socially or professionally, or not, society is still uncomfortable with women who kill. Yet, at the same time, it is fascinated by them. Violent crimes that lead to murder are still rare, so is this why it is still so shocking when women become serial killers, murder their family members and children, or use their position of trust to kill?

What may be fuelling this "shock" factor could stem from Victorian values when women were deemed virtuous, prudent and full of piety. They were expected to show devotion to family by honouring their parents, their husbands and wider family members. Sex before marriage was definitely out, and attending church at least once a week and being devoted to Christian worship, were prerequisites for the Victorian woman. No swearing, no mention of needing to use the bathroom and no nudity were the rules of the day. A woman could be considered lewd if she even dared show her lower leg to a man. Women were seen as necessary for inspiring and supporting men, serving them and bearing their children. They were generally kept inside where they could be protected from immoral influences. It was an economic, political and civil culture where women lived to serve, and violent crimes of the earlier centuries, and those yet to come, were out of reach of women in the latter half of the 1800s. However, there are those that advocated, and still do, that Jack the Ripper could have been a woman.

In Australia, Professor Ian Findlay used powerful DNA profiling techniques to examine the 118-year-old letters in 2006, which revealed that the Ripper could, in fact, have been a woman. He said: "This is the most sophisticated DNA fingerprinting technique in the world, but the sample doesn't give us enough evidence to pinpoint the killer. However, there is an interesting twist because we do know this sample is likely to be a female sample." Interestingly, Frederick Abberline was the one man who thought the Ripper could be a woman. His boss doubted that a woman could be capable of such atrocious crimes, but Abberline remained unconvinced. The chief suspect was Mary Pearcey, born in 1866. She was executed at the scaffold in 1890 after being convicted of murdering her lover's wife and baby daughter. These murders bore striking similarities to the Ripper killings. Pearcey was extremely strong, with nerves of "iron cast", according to reports. No one can be certain of anything without hard evidence, but one thing is for sure, the case of Jack the Ripper remains one of the greatest murder mysteries of all time. The fact that the Ripper could have been a woman makes the story even more compelling.

Of course, during the Victorian era of the late 19th century mental illness was not recognized in the same way that it would be today. It was firmly believed that if a woman was not influenced by outside forces there could be no exposure to the "evils" that continued on the streets of large cities. The fact that in 1890 a woman might be under severe mental stress given the circumstances within her own home, or suffering from mental illness, lust or greed, would never even have been considered a possibility. It's also likely that confined to their homes, dressed in unsuitable attire – despite it being the fashion and accepted dress code – while being devoid of all exercise, also played a part in why women were deemed non-criminal. They literally wouldn't have had the physical strength, or so commentators believed. It is likely that these beliefs and limited understanding with regard to individuals of a bygone era are what lie at the heart of why society today finds it difficult to comprehend how women can kill.

Those women who did manage to commit violent crimes in the late 1800s were either given more lenient sentences, or were given harsher ones, than men. Criminality was linked to sexual perversion, and a Victorian woman was expected to suppress her sexuality. The underbelly of society was deemed to be where violent crimes were carried out, by an "ungodly" unclean lower class. There was even a criminal class all of its own. These people were "wretched" according to those of upper- and middle-class standing; and the class system was the driving factor behind almost every facet of life at this time. Women from lower classes would be treated harshly, and their "depraved" circumstances blamed for their crimes. Madness would be cited as the reason for a woman of "good standing" to have committed a crime. Unlike lower-class women, who found themselves in prison, well-bred women were sent to institutions, or confined to some part of the family home. Apart from a select few, whose observations were overlooked, at no time was it recognized that women were equally as capable of violent crime as men. Victorian values placed women among the ranks of "moral beings" incapable of depravity unless forced into it or found to be completely "mad".

This continued to some extent into the first half of the 20th century, when women charged with offences were considered misguided and in need of help. In the 1930s, offenders were deemed "delinquent" and a "good" match in marriage was considered likely to prevent further offences. Society, unable to imagine the horrors that a woman could mete out, continued to justify crimes committed by them. Post-natal, pre-menstrual and defence against male aggressors were all deemed plausible excuses for women who "clearly couldn't help themselves" when it came to committing a violent act. Yet, during war years, it was perfectly acceptable for a woman to kill, if necessary, as long as she returned to her virtuous and pious life afterwards. Women continued to be stereotyped. Even in the 1970s, young children, both girls and boys, were brought up on the nursery rhymes dating back hundreds of years. The rhyme "What are little boys made of" can be traced to the early 1800s and indicates that the "battle of the sexes" is an old story. The words to the nursery rhyme suggest that little boys were made of "snips and snails and puppy dog tails", while little girls were made of "sugar and spice and all things nice", so no wonder the Victorians heralded the female gender as more "moral" and "elevated" than the male. However, women are quite as capable of killing for lust, sexual exploitation, jealousy, greed, revenge, psychotic reasons, financial gain and self-defence as men – it's just that less do. Sometimes, women will hire someone to do their "dirty work" for them. It makes them no less guilty of murder. It is suggested that women who hire hitmen are more likely to be motivated by greed and the financial gain from which they will benefit once the victim is murdered. These women are often detected by the tell-tale "celebration" that might follow this type of murder – for example, getting their hair done and going out for dinner in the weeks after the death of a husband or lover. Many experts cite that no women truly experiencing grief is likely to do either of these things. Poison has often been the weapon of choice for women who murder. It was a common form of ridding a woman of a husband or lovers that were "surplus to requirements", especially during the 16th and 17th centuries. Women who killed in this way included Lucrezia Borgia, and Catherine de' Medici, who killed her political adversaries, but poisoning was a practice that continued into the 20th century. Poison was a favourable method of killing because no physical strength was required, and the substance itself was often tasteless and left no traces.

Just outside the tiny hamlet of Ellwood in the Forest of Dean in Gloucestershire is a white isolated dwelling, nestling in a tiny valley on the old Coleford to Parkend railway, known locally as the "murder house". In 1928, Beatrice Annie Pace became a household name when she stood trial for the murder of her husband, by poisoning, with whom she had shared a house on Fetter Hill. There was a wave of public sympathy for the mother of five, and the public was so convinced of her innocence that literally hundreds of people contributed to a fund to pay for her defence barrister. The trial took place in Shire Hall, Gloucester, where crowds gathered to show their support for the accused woman. The judge decided that there just wasn't enough evidence to convict Beatrice Pace of the murder of Harry Pace, 36, a Gloucestershire quarryman and sheep farmer, with arsenic. He ordered that the jury find Beatrice not guilty.

Harry had died following an agonizing illness, but it was the fact that the police investigating decided a post-mortem was necessary that brought the case to public attention. There were rumours of extramarital affairs and hidden money, as well as accusations that

Beatrice had used arsenic to poison her husband. It transpired that Harry Pace had died from a large dose of arsenic and the police needed to find out whether it was accidental, suicide or murder. Beatrice naturally fell under the spotlight. With insufficient evidence against her, she was acquitted in July 1928. She moved to Gloucester, Wales and eventually Stroud to avoid the glare of the media, but whether she murdered her husband or not is still up for debate with some. While many believed, and still do, that the kindly grandmother was incapable of poisoning her husband – who dipped his sheep in an arsenic solution to treat them – there are others who remain unsure. Even in 2013, some 40 years after Beatrice's death, there are locals that still refer to the dwelling on Fetter Hill as the "murder house" and to the hidden money blocked up in the brickwork, of which there is no proof. Whatever the truth, in 1928 Beatrice Pace became a household name, and was given celebrity status in much the same way that those in the media are given in the 21st century. If she had been found guilty, she would have faced the hangman's noose. Interestingly, capital punishment hadn't been meted out in Britain for women since 1907, although in 1922, just six years before the "murder" of Harry Pace, things began to change for women.

Since 1907, a vast movement in favour of women's "equality" had made great strides. Women were militantly on their way to gaining the vote, they gained places in Parliament, and a small number had become magistrates, barristers and solicitors. Women jurors had also become more commonplace, and one was amongst those that condemned a woman named Edith Thompson to death. Two other women were also condemned in the same way in 1922. The move to endorse equality for women went against the 1922 "plea" that women "should not be equal with men", and the *Mirror* wrote in December that year that it was "a question of punishment instead of privilege". Even though Mrs Thompson was given the death penalty there were many that didn't think she would suffer the hangman's noose "because she [is] a woman". However, the jury took the view that she was as guilty as the man with her who "struck the blows". The *Mirror* wrote: "If no new interpretation of the evidence is accepted on appeal, then, there can be no conceivable reason for remitting the penalty in this case unless we determine to accept the 'unwritten law' that no woman is ever to be hanged." It continued: "We do not much like the idea of 'unwritten laws'. That is a phrase generally equivalent to 'popular sentimentality'. In this case we must not argue either for or against the application of the death penalty to the woman concerned. But it is worth remarking that if the unwritten law takes effect it will mean that no woman will ever be hanged again." The article finished with the words: "In that case, let us write the law and accept the consequences of the abolition of capital punishment for women. This will save judges the vain ceremony of condemning those who are bound to be reprieved on the plea of pity."

Of course, the death penalty in Britain was carried out after 1922. On 13th July 1955, convicted murderer Ruth Ellis faced the gallows. Just one year before, the *Mirror* had asked: "What makes a woman want to kill …?" The article was in response to the case of Mrs Christofi, from Cyprus, who faced the gallows on 15th December 1954 at Holloway in London. She was the 14th woman to be hanged in Britain since 1900. During the same period, 1,168 men had been sent to the gallows across the country. The newspaper wrote that a man was far more likely to murder than a woman. Men also ran a much higher risk of being hung for their crimes. In 1954, statistics showed that around one male murderer in two could expect a reprieve, while the number was much greater for women, with around nine murderers in 10 being "let off" the death penalty. However, the paper stated that many of those women who killed were mothers of new babies; such a woman was deemed "out of her mind at the time". It seemed in the mid-20th century that opinions hadn't changed very much. The paper cited that women who were found guilty of murdering their newborn babies were "not responsible" for what they did. However, the paper asked their readers to put cases of infanticide aside and consider what really turned a woman into a murderer.

Four of the women who went to the gallows before Mrs Christofi were "baby farmers", that is, women who took in the infants of others as a business, but ended up killing them. (Although forms of adoption and fostering have occurred throughout history, modern-day practices did not exist in the way they are recognized today until the late 1920s.) The last woman who worked as a baby farmer and who killed a child in her care was executed in 1903. Five of the 13 women who had suffered the death penalty since

1900 had killed their husbands. The remainder had been found guilty of killing other women, including a landlady. Mrs Christofi was convicted of murdering her daughter-in-law. Interestingly, women who used poison – therefore meaning the murders were premeditated – were less likely to gain a reprieve. According to the *Mirror* in 1954, the older a woman became, the less likely she was to kill. Edith Thompson was 28, while Mrs Christofi was the oldest murderer in the first half of the 20th century at 53. The paper said: "While women don't often murder, they are very often the cause of murder. Most of the men who get hanged go to the gallows either because they killed women or because they killed other men in disputes over women." The newspaper article also said: "A man is far more likely to kill his wife than the other way round. It seems that when a husband is angry he may become murderous, but when a wife is angry she just nags. Again, looking at the figures for this century, not one woman since 1900 has killed in drink, or in a drunken quarrel, or in the course of a fight. Nor has a woman ever shot a policeman. All those kinds of murder," stated the paper, "are a male monopoly."

During the latter part of the 20th century poison became a less likely murder weapon of choice when technology advanced to such a stage, alongside forensic evidence, that it became virtually impossible to use poison to kill. Today, more than 2,000 poisons can be traced under a spectroscope.

Some women who find themselves in an impossible situation may end up killing. Women who are victims of domestic abuse may reach a point of no return after many months and even years of suffering at the hands of a husband or partner. It's difficult to understand why women who are abused don't leave their abusers, but these women are often "groomed" to the point where they are reliant on the perpetrator. Psychological abuse is just as damaging, if not more so in some cases, than physical. That might be hard to comprehend, but a woman who has children with her attacker may have been subjected to the most frightening and humiliating of ordeals, yet stay because not only will her abuser not allow her to leave the home with her children, he has probably already persuaded her that she has nowhere to go and that no one will believe her. Abusive men come from all races and backgrounds. An abuser is just as likely to have come from a privileged background as a poor one. The abused women, who are often vulnerable before they begin these types of relationships, believe that there is no way out. For some, the only option is to kill or fear being killed, especially where they feel their children are at risk. For centuries it was acceptable for a man to beat and chastise his wife – it was a part of life, as the woman in a relationship was subservient to her husband. She had to promise to "obey" him when they married: he was the breadwinner and she had little choice but to live by his rules. Should she break those rules, then she could expect to be punished, sometimes severely. It wasn't illegal for a man to rape his wife until 1991 in Britain, and 1993 in the United States. It's hard to imagine in the 21st century that women had very little say as to what happened to them as individuals for many hundreds of years. But abused women still bear the brunt of controlling, manipulative behaviours, which are often underlined by lies, violence and terror. Many women who end up killing their abusers do so in self-defence. They then end up in a particularly difficult situation in court, where they have to prove beyond doubt that their life was in immediate danger and that force was necessary to avoid unlawful bodily harm. While more is known about domestic violence today, it has taken a long time for the judicial system to recognize that women in these relationships are well and truly trapped. However, a very small percentage of women in abusive relationships actually go on to kill, and usually only as a result of extreme circumstances and danger.

Other women who kill include those who turn to violent crime for financial gain: some may hire hitmen but others "do it themselves". Love and lust are other motives behind female murder, as are mental illness and sexual fantasy. Jane Toppan was a nurse with a troubled childhood who preyed on weak, ill patients. She gained extreme sexual pleasure from taking patients in her care to the brink of death with drugs, before reviving them and repeating the pattern. Her "Angel of Death" mission began in 1885 and ended when she was charged and convicted of the deaths of 11 patients. She admitted to 31 killings in total, but was found not guilty by reason of insanity and was sent to an asylum in her native United States. Belle Gunness was an equally murderous woman whose greed drove her to kill around 42 victims, including her own two daughters. Once a family member was dead, Gunness collected

Women Killers

the insurance money and began life anew. After the murders of her children and husband, she began luring wealthy middle-aged men with adverts. Under the pretence of looking for love, Gunness then poisoned the unsuspecting victims before cashing in. She was reported to have died in a fire, set deliberately, at her farmhouse, but some believe the charred remains were not those of the "Black Widow". Towards the end of the 20th century, two women hit the headlines in America after they were found guilty of the deaths of their own children – all because of failed relationships that they were desperate to hold on to. Susan Smith suffered a number of personality disorders, which led to the deaths of her young sons, Michael aged three and Alex, 14 months. Smith's lover made it clear that their relationship was over, but she just couldn't believe that he'd left her. Thinking that if she didn't have any children her wealthy lover would return, she drove to the edge of a South Carolina lake with her sleeping sons in the back of the vehicle in 1994. She got out of the car, put it in drive and stood and watched as it rolled into the depths of the lake. The ruthless killer then phoned police and blamed the crime on an unknown assailant. However, after separating lies from cold hard facts the police realized that Smith was guilty. She was convicted and sentenced to 30 years behind bars. Eleven years earlier, in May 1983, Diane Downs had shot her three children at point-blank range. Downs' lover had told her that a relationship that included children was not part of his long-term plan, and the deluded woman concocted a plot that would leave her child-free. In truth, the relationship had been turning sour for some time, but, in an effort to keep her man, Downs stopped her car along a deserted stretch of road and shot Christie, eight, Cheryl, seven, and three-year-old Danny. Cheryl died at the scene, but Downs took Christie and Danny to the emergency room where they fought for their lives. Christie was paralysed on one side of her body and left with speech difficulties. Danny was paralysed from the waist down. Christie displayed remarkable bravery when she told the courtroom at Downs' trial how her mother had shot all three children. Downs was given a life sentence plus 50 years, but became eligible for parole in 2008. It was denied. Parole was denied again in 2010. Downs continues to state her innocence. It was a story that shook not just the United States, but the rest of the world too. A few, however, still believe Downs did not commit the crime.

Severe mental illness has had a part to play in violent crime. Narcissism and schizophrenia are just two personality disorders which have led to murder. Andrea Yates killed her five children by drowning them in the bath at the family home in Texas, in 2001. She was suffering from severe post-natal depression and psychosis. There had been many signs that Yates was suffering from serious mental illness, as she had had a number of psychotic episodes and suicide attempts, and it has been cited by some that she is clinically insane. At a retrial in 2006, Yates was found not guilty by reason of insanity. A convicted murderer who did not reach the category of "insane" was Canadian killer Karla Homolka, who, together with her husband, Paul Bernardo, kidnapped, raped and murdered three young women, including her own sister. Homolka showed no mercy for these young victims, whom she imprisoned in her own home. She eventually cut a deal with the authorities in order to secure a lesser sentence, by telling them everything they needed to know about Bernardo, who was eventually identified as the notorious "Scarborough Rapist". While Homolka claimed she was just as much a victim of Bernardo as other women, psychologists believe that she displayed signs of psychopathy, which she hid well under a façade. The videos of the young victims, which the couple filmed, showed Homolka readily taking part in the crimes. It all began when Bernardo took a fancy to Homolka's teenage sister who was still a virgin. The young girl was plied with drink and drugs at a family Christmas party before being raped by her sister's then fiancé. She tragically died from choking on her own vomit – this was to lead to the deaths of the other victims as Bernardo felt that his "present" from Homolka had been ruined.

Unlike killers such as Homolka, most women murderers are much more subtle in their crimes than their male counterparts. Often calculating, sly and underhand, these women commit murder "quietly" and blend into society as "normal" people, whom most would not suspect of being capable of cold-blooded murder. Such women are deliberate in their actions, and domestic "accidents" and poison have tended, throughout history, to be the modus operandi of choice. However, women who kill tend to fall into a number of different groups, including "Black Widows", who murder almost entirely for profit, but don't necessarily limit themselves to husbands as victims. Sons, daughters, parents and other extended family members may fall victim to Black Widows, although experts agree that carefully targeted strangers are also now becoming more attractive in killing sprees, such is the driving force behind greed- and "profit"-motivated murders. However, experts also cite that sexually motivated murder is not particularly within the remit of women killers. Men, on the other hand, usually kill in a sexually motivated crime and will face their victim one on one in order to gain arousal and sexual gratification during a murder. Women tend to be close to their victims, while men are more likely to stalk strangers and use physical strength to perpetrate murder. Women are more likely to use non-aggressive forms of killing, largely for motives such as control and manipulation, revenge and profit. Women who kill more than once often tend to "get away with it" for much longer than a man intent on serial killing because of their tendency to be more subtle; however, both men and women who kill are psychopaths in the sense that they lack a conscience. Victims are seen as a means to an end – there is no compassion, no remorse. "Angels of Death" or "mercy killers" are also more likely to be women. Some, like Homolka, are sexual predators, although these women killers are rare, while others may be revenge killers. Insanity can be attributed to some female killers, but in other cases motives and drive are undefined. Authorities the world over believe that a number of unsolved crimes, or cold cases, may be attributable to women. Homolka was part of a "team", like Myra Hindley and Rosemary "Rose" West: such women form a bond with a male counterpart and their main role is to support, encourage and incite, as well as taking part in sexually motivated killings. Hate is strongly linked to sexually motivated murders, whether the victims are men, women or children. Many women who kill are obsessive and jealous, and while murderers like Martha Wise from Ohio only killed once she reached her forties, many females tend to be in their twenties and thirties. Some women team up with another woman to carry out their crimes, and others may work in a "family" group – including Sara Aldrete, who worked as part of a cult in Mexico and was responsible for human "sacrifices" during her time as "La Madrina". It is more likely that women who commit violent crimes as part of a team will inflict considerable pain and suffering on the victim of a bloody nature, including torture. Those who kill alone are prone to work quietly and subtly: the victim is unlikely to know what's about to happen to them.

This book takes a disturbing look at the minds and crimes of some of the world's worst female serial killers, as well as those that managed to defy and evade the authorities, resulting in the deaths of vulnerable children at the hands of their own mothers or female family members.

Florence Maybrick

1889

In 1904, Florence Maybrick was released from a female convict prison in Aylesbury, where she had been incarcerated for many years. She had been condemned to death for the murder of her husband in 1889, but the sentence was commuted to penal servitude for life – generally meaning a term of 20 years – for good behaviour. The American-born prisoner owed her release largely to influence from the United States, where thousands of people, convinced of her innocence, had made many attempts to see her set free. The matter had been raised in the House of Commons on more than one occasion and several appeals had been made by the American Secretary of State, while Mr Choate, the American Ambassador, had made a number of diplomatic representations. In addition, there were private petitions from across the Atlantic and a "Women's International Maybrick Association" had been formed.

Florence Maybrick was young, attractive and well connected at the time of her husband's death. There was also an element of doubt as to whether she was actually guilty of murder. Her mother, Baroness von Roques, was responsible for a number of important lawsuits, which involved immense tracts of land in Kentucky, Virginia and West Virginia, covering more than two and a half million acres at an estimated value of £1.5 million – an extremely substantial amount of money at the beginning of the

20th century. She cited that unless her daughter could be produced as a witness in legal proceedings, she herself would lose all claim to the land. So Maybrick's release was granted on special licence. After thanking the governor of the prison, Maybrick left Aylesbury in a carriage with her mother, bound for a private house just outside London. Inside prison, the convicted women had been given heavy laundry duties, but, once released, she returned to a charmed life of privilege. Imprisoned at the age of 28, Maybrick was 42 when she was released in 1904, after 14 years.

On a spring day in 1889, James Maybrick from Liverpool was taken ill after attending the races at Wirral. He died on 11th May that year and his wife was arrested and charged with poisoning him. The day before his death, Florence had fallen ill herself after 12 days at his bedside. She had woken 36 hours later to find her husband had died. In fact, she was still lying ill in bed when the police arrested her. She was too ill to attend the police court and the magistrate and court officials were called to her bedroom to indict the charge and detain her on remand. When the remand date arrived Florence was still too ill to attend, but, in the meantime, the coroner's jury had sat on the case – the dead man's body had been exhumed in the dead of night – and a verdict of "Wilful Murder" was returned. The trial began on 31st July 1889 and lasted a week. By the time of her release, the authorities seemed to want to keep the latest news with regard to Florence Maybrick shrouded in mystery, much to journalists' frustrations.

Despite the lawsuits on the other side of the Atlantic, it

appeared that Florence would remain in Britain for the foreseeable future, while reports stated that the amount of arsenic found in the body of her deceased husband was just one-tenth of a grain. It was such a minute quantity that reporters cited it "would not have caused the death of even a mouse, and certainly not that of a man". Meanwhile, it was revealed that the Maybrick children, aged 20 and 16 in 1904, had been "adopted" by a "loving family", following their mother's incarceration. They were reported not to have known at this time that the woman about whom they were reading in the newspapers was their own mother. Florence Maybrick moved just 20 miles outside Liverpool where she was said to be under supervision, according to newspaper reports in February 1904, but two weeks later it was established that she had been tracked down by the *Mirror*. She was, in actual fact, located as a "visitor" in the Church of England Sisterhood of the Epiphany in Truro, Cornwall, after intervention by the Duchess of Bedford. Her remaining months of her life sentence were being lived out in a simple cloister overlooking the cathedral city. The newspaper also cited that they understood that none of the Sisters of the Epiphany knew of the past of the visitor currently residing in their long Tudor-style building. However, many doubt that as true. Rules for Mrs Maybrick included no access to newspapers and being in bed by 9.00pm. All inquiries were warded off by the Mother Superior who was entirely responsible for the woman's well-being and safe keeping. However, despite still serving part of her life sentence, Florence had been granted permission to attend services at Truro cathedral and to wander the city's sleepy narrow streets. Her sentence was to finish on 30th July 1904, after serving 15 years. Throughout her incarceration Florence Maybrick appealed to the authorities for a reinvestigation of her case and a new trial so that evidence suppressed at her original trial could establish her innocence, but a lack of a Court of Criminal Appeal made a subsequent retrial nigh on impossible.

In July 1904, it was announced through the *Mirror* that "the case of Mrs Maybrick is to be revived with the object of securing for her a free pardon through the graciousness of King Edward". Even President Roosevelt was expected to signify his sympathy with the woman by signing a petition in the United States. Her counsel added: "Imagine a young, beautiful woman, the mother of two fine children, spending 15 years in a convict prison, conscious all the while that she is guiltless of the charge put upon her. Then recollect that she has earned in gaol a clean record for good conduct, and you have a remarkable picture of feminine fortitude and patience." It then came to light that James Maybrick had been in the habit of "dosing" himself on various poisonous drugs. Each of the drugs, if taken to excess, was sufficient to produce an inflammatory condition of the internal organs, irrespective of arsenic. In fact, 21 irritant poisons had been administered to James Maybrick within six days prior to his death, prescribed by doctors. They included cocaine, morphia, arsenic in a form of Fowler's solution, as well as nux vomica, henbane and jaborandi. Even the Home Secretary stated in July 1904 that there was "reasonable doubt" as to whether Florence had caused her husband's death by arsenic poisoning, and the Home Office Analyst recorded his conviction that she was not guilty. However, even after her permanent release towards the end of July, the papers were still asking if she was innocent. There had been fallings out in the marital home, James Maybrick had admonished and hit his wife, and there was gossip from former servants. Florence Maybrick, meanwhile, travelled to France to spend time with her mother in Rouen. She eventually returned to America, and in May 1905, Mr Choate, the American Ambassador in London, confirmed that the British authorities had refused further clemency in the case of Florence Maybrick. There would be no pardon. She died in the United States in October 1941 at the age of 80.

Madame Giriat

1903

Despite calls of "Death to the murderess" by members of a large crowd that gathered, Madame Giriat was unperturbed as she was taken from Chambéry prison on 14th November 1903 to participate in a "reconstitution of the crime". Unshaken by the hostility, Madame Giriat walked out of the police station to a waiting van, and showed the same reserved calm during the reconstruction. On 20th September 1903, Eugénie Fougère, described as a "professional beauty", was murdered at her villa in Aix-les-Bains. Victorine Giriat, her companion, and Henri Bassot, the victim's lover, stood before judge and jury on 3rd June 1904 accused of her murder.

It was a "romance of crime", according to the newspapers, where the young, rich victim had jewels that "astonished the boulevards", while her "reticule", filled with 1,000 franc notes, was "proverbial". Giriat accompanied Eugénie Fougère to Aix "to take the cure" as her maid, but on the morning of 20th September Fougère was found strangled, while the companion was found bound and gagged. Lucie Marie, Fougère's servant, was also found dead. Giriat gave a moving account of how the killer had also tried to murder her, and stated that jewels and notes worth a great deal had disappeared. Eventually, following an intense police investigation, Giriat and Bassot stood in the dock. Bassot, from Vichy, was charged with arranging the murder, and Madame

Giriat with aiding the "hit man" hired for the crime – a man named Ladermann, who committed suicide before the case came to trial. Giriat stood up well to cross-examination. The woman, in her forties, defended herself fiercely and wasn't at all perturbed by the fact that Bassot revealed himself to be a faithless lover – despite the president of the court accusing her of allowing herself to be bound and gagged. She asked the court: "If you had been in my place, I should like to know what you would have done?" The first witness in the case was hairdresser Monsieur Pelletier, who was one of the first to discover the bodies, and who thought Giriat's attitude was suspicious. Two doctors, Coze and Remi, both told the court they believed Fougère had been killed in her sleep by at least two people and the case was adjourned.

It was one of the most sensational cases in France at the time, and it came to an end on 5th June 1904. Giriat received 15 years in prison for her part in the double murder, while Bassot was given 10 years. Another man, charged and convicted of receiving stolen goods, Robardet, was given three months. During the trial, the jury heard how Fougère had been strangled on her bed, as had her servant, Lucie Marie. It transpired that, before his suicide, Ladermann had written a confessional note, which implicated both Giriat and Bassot. It was decided that despite Giriat being "extremely ugly" Bassot had taken the maid as his lover, with the intention of inciting her to take part in the murders in order to gain substantial wealth. However, one of the jewels, reported to be worth F3,000, was sold by Robardet for just six francs and 75 cents. Bassot had asked Giriat: "Have you no rich girl friends we can do for?", and after an acquaintance with Fougère had been made, he wrote, "We must do for Fougère. I will send you a sure man who will do it." Ladermann was admitted to the villa by Giriat while the victims were out. After all three women had fallen asleep Giriat stated: "I was awakened suddenly … the man opened my door and blew out my light. 'Quick,' he said." She asked about the servant and Ladermann replied: "Done for." Giriat then stated that the man hadn't answered when she asked directly about Fougère, and described how she had lost consciousness as he covered her mouth with his hand and told her: "… be a brave woman".

Bassot declared himself innocent of any involvement in the double murder and attack on Giriat, but said he'd had a relationship with the maid as a passing amusement, before telling the court how ugly he thought she was. He then accused Giriat of implementing him in a crime that he had had nothing to do with. Both the accused screamed at each other in court, claiming that the other was a liar. However, the screaming "quarrel" that ensued between the former lovers was to reveal vital evidence – and the shouting match actually led to them both confirming their parts in the murders.

Jeanne Weber

1905

Less than a year after Giriat and Bassot were found guilty of murder, a mother in the Rue-Pre-Mandit in Paris, France, was accused of murdering a number of children. Her own brother and sister-in-law alleged that she had strangled their four children, and attempted to murder a fifth child. Weber's own two children were already dead, and her brother, Charles Weber, claimed that his sister had been driven "insane" by their deaths. He accused Jeanne of "enticing parents to lend her the company of their offspring in her lonely state, and then murdering the little ones by choking them". The police had launched an investigation into the murders by April 1905, but Jeanne's husband was distraught, claiming: "She was so sweet when I married her." In May 1908, when Jeanne Weber was accused of the murder of a child, newspapers reported that she had been dubbed "the Ogress" due to the number of children who had mysteriously met their deaths at her hands. There was "damning evidence" that she had strangled a six-year-old boy at Comercy, and she was accused of "homicidal mania". It came to light that Weber was suspected of killing children as far back as 1901 – when she murdered her own child – before murdering her two-year-old niece Georgette (who died in her lap). A few days later, the little girl's sister, Suzanne, died in similar circumstances. The bodies of both children showed signs of strangulation; however, up to this point, the doctors involved in the cases had believed that the deaths were natural. After being asked to move out by her distraught brother and sister-in-law, she moved in with a second sister-in-law, who discovered her own two little children dead in mysterious circumstances within four days of Weber's arrival. Both bodies bore the same marks and both deaths occurred when the children's parents were absent. A week later, another nephew, the son of another sister-in-law, was found dead. Jeanne Weber was arrested and tried, but acquitted. She next murdered the young daughter of a farmer who befriended her after the trial, and for a time the murders ceased.

Jeanne Weber disappeared for a while after that, but reappeared in Comercy, where she was given lodgings by an innkeeper, M Poirot and his wife. The couple were unaware of the woman's identity and allowed their six-year-old to sleep in Weber's bed after she told them she was lonely. At around 1.00am one Saturday morning, a woman called Madame Guvilet, sleeping in an adjoining room, heard the boy's plaintive and smothered cries. She woke the child's parents, claiming something was very wrong. They went into Weber's room where they found their son lying in her arms, dead. He had been strangled.

Most reports with regard to Weber state that she began murdering in March 1905, with the killing of her niece Georgette; however, newspaper reports from 1908 claim the killings began much earlier, with two of her own three children in 1901. These deaths were unexplained, but doctors regarded the cause to be natural, due to illness. In fact, many of the deaths were explained away as illnesses, including typhoid, diphtheria and "convulsions", before Weber's true "madness" was exposed in 1908. Other reports also point to the fact that Weber killed prior to 1905. What is clear is that her killing spree began in earnest in 1905 and that, having killed her two young nieces, she then took the life of her own son in order to allay suspicion. This points to the fact that Weber was not mentally insane; although the jury at her first trial just could not believe that a grieving mother could commit the atrocities of which she was accused. Weber's last victim was found with bulging eyes and blood down his nightshirt. The young child had bitten his tongue as he died. Weber, at last, was brought to justice. She managed to convince the jury that she was insane and the judge sentenced her to life imprisonment in 1908. She was found dead in prison two years later, having taken her own life.

Edith Thompson
(with Frederick Bywaters)

1922

Scotland Yard detectives were called in to "unravel a mysterious crime" that was committed in Belgrave Road, Ilford, in Essex, just after midnight on 4th October 1922. Residents were woken by a woman screaming, and in response to loud knocking on his front door, Dr Maudsley went outside and found Percy Thompson, 33, a shipbroker's clerk, dead on the pavement. Mrs Thompson, who was with her husband at the time, stated that she saw no one attack him, but a detailed examination revealed more than 12 wounds to the victim's head, neck and right arm, which had been inflicted with a sharp instrument. It was clear to the police that the man had been murdered. The couple had been within yards of their home in Kensington Gardens when the murder occurred. Chief Detective Inspector Wensley of Scotland Yard, who headed the case, worked with Ilford Borough Council officials to dredge a number of drains near the crime scene, with the hope of finding the murder weapon. Their efforts proved fruitless.

John Weber, who lived near the murder scene, told the *Mirror*: "About 12.30am I was on my way upstairs to bed when I heard a woman several times scream, 'Don't! Don't! Don't!' I ran to the front door and saw in the distance a tall man and two women. One of the women I now understand to have been Mrs Thompson." The couple had stopped on the corner of Kensington Gardens. When Weber went outside he saw a man bleeding from his mouth. Dr Maudsley added that he: "saw a man on the pavement. He was in a sitting position propped up against the wall of a house. He had no hat on, and his head had fallen forward. He appeared to be bleeding from the mouth and was dead. His wife was standing near him and seemed to be very distressed and hysterical, and I could get no clear account of what had happened." The doctor had only examined the man by the light of matches and so hadn't seen the puncture wound to Thompson's throat.

The following day, Percy Thompson's wife, Edith, known as Edie, was charged with his murder, along with Frederick Bywaters, 20, a ship's steward from Upper Norwood. They were due to appear at Stratford Police Court on 6th October, as the post-mortem report of the murder victim's numerous wounds revealed that he had been stabbed with a pair of scissors. Wensley and Divisional Inspector Francis Hall had had a long interview with the distressed woman the day before: as a result of which they then charged her with murder.

The following statement was made by Edie Thompson and put forward as evidence – it read: "We had no quarrel. We were quite happy together. I did not see anybody about at the time. My husband and I were talking about going to a dance." The couple had been on their way back from the theatre – where they went regularly – and Mrs Thompson was known to have loved dancing. Bywaters entered the police court first, where crowds of people had gathered, while Thompson appeared in what she'd been wearing two nights earlier when her husband was murdered. Two days later there was a "dramatic development", when an important clue was discovered: a bloodstained dagger between eight and 10 inches was found in a sewer in Seymour Gardens, just around the corner from the murder scene.

Percy Thompson's funeral took place on 10th October 1922 at the City of London cemetery, but only a few mourners and friends were admitted to the building. A day later, Frederick Bywaters stated in court: "I love her, and could not go on seeing her lead that life. He always seemed several degrees less than a snake. I did not intend to kill him. I only meant to injure him." The dramatic statement continued by Bywaters saying that he had taken his knife from his pocket and the two men fought, before "Thompson got the worst of it". The court also heard how Bywaters had been a paying guest of the Thompsons and that the trio knew each other "very well indeed", according to the prosecutor, Mr Lewis. Meanwhile, Bywaters' statement said that Percy Thompson was an abusive man who did not treat his wife properly. She had been in the habit of meeting up with Frederick Bywaters. Sometimes her husband knew of their meetings, and sometimes he didn't. Bywaters also stated that he had known for a long time that Edie Thompson was trapped in an unhappy marriage. This was confirmed by Percy's brother, Richard Thompson, in court, as he also claimed that the couple had had an unhappy union. When the inquest resumed on 20th October, Edie Thompson was in the Holloway infirmary. Letters, stated Francis Hall, would be used to provide further evidence in the case. However, the coroner refused to read the letters by Thompson to Bywaters, and a verdict of wilful murder was returned against the young man. The coroner also stated that, apart from the letters, there was no evidence against Mrs Thompson. Even Bywaters had stated that she knew nothing of the attack he had planned on Percy Thompson. The coroner said that he did have suspicions with regard to the contents of the letters, but that: "The police did quite right in arresting this woman, but there is no definite evidence beyond the letters to show she has instigated this man." The jury found that Percy Thompson met his death as a result of a stab wound inflicted by Bywaters.

On 24th October, when the couple were jointly charged in connection with the victim's death, the letters were read out in a Stratford court. References to poison appeared in several communiqués, and in one, Thompson wrote: "You said it was enough for an elephant." In another she wrote: "Be jealous so much that you will do something desperate." Thompson collapsed as the letters were read. Her counsel, Mr Stern, objected to the letters being used in evidence. Another letter read out stated: "Come and see me on Monday lunchtime. He suspects – Peidi." Thompson had also sent Bywaters cuttings from the case of a local doctor who had wanted a divorce, and where things had escalated badly. She wrote to him implying that she wanted to poison her husband – she even intimated a number of times that she had tried, but that nothing had happened. She wrote: "Oh, darling, I do feel so down and unhappy. Would not the stuff make some small pills coated with soap and dipped in liquorice powder? I know I feel I shall never get him to take a sufficient quantity of anything bitter." It continued: "All that lying and scheming and subterfuge to obtain one little hour in each day – when by right of nature and our love we should be together for all the twenty-four in every day." Thompson collapsed several times as her words were read out and on one occasion had to be removed from court. The court also heard: "It must be remembered that digitalin is an emulative poison, and that the same dose is harmless if taken once, yet frequently repeated becomes deadly." These words were quoted by Thompson from a book about belladonna to Bywaters.

From the letters it was clear that Edith Thompson was completely in love with Frederick "Freddie" Bywaters, but she also made it clear that she was trying to be a dutiful wife who was "bent to the will of her husband". Stern argued that all the newspaper cuttings and quotes from publications may not have a sinister meaning and the inquest continued. There were around 50 cuttings contained in various letters, which even the police had to admit ranged over a variety of subjects. But the chairman of the inquest said: "I understand there are grave reasons why a remand should be given. You know I expressed my opinion on the undesirability of spinning out this case, but I understand that it is really necessary. A case we expected to be such a simple and short one has become very complicated." While the letters were read out, Thompson hung her head. Bywaters, who for the most part looked expressionless, also looked tense as the evidence was laid before the court in black and white.

In early November 1922, the grave of Percy Thompson was exhumed so that his body could be re-examined. The utmost secrecy was "observed in connection with the exhumation of the body", which was then examined by Spilsbury, the former Home Office specialist. Meanwhile, the prisoners remained on remand. Police inquiries were still ongoing in mid-November, but by 24th of the month, the whole of Britain woke to the news that traces of poison had been discovered in Percy's body. It meant new charges against Edith Thompson, and both she and Bywaters were committed for trial on a charge of murder. The new charges were that between 1st June and 4th October "she administered poison", and "solicited and proposed" to Bywaters that he murder Thompson, and so "solicited and incited Bywaters to conspire and agree with her to murder Thompson". Traces of morphine were found in the victim's system. Twenty-seven-year-old Thompson looked ashen as the charges were brought. The KC leading the prosecution at the Old Bailey was the Solicitor General, Mr J W H Inskip, who was to be assisted by Travers Humphreys and Roland Oliver. Cecil Whiteley, KC, and Huntly Jenkins were assigned to defend Bywaters, while Thompson was to be defended by Sir Henry Curtis Bennett, KC, and Walter Frampton. The judge was named as Mr Justice Shearman.

The December Sessions of the Central Criminal Court at the Old Bailey were opened by the Lord Mayor, attended by the sheriffs and under sheriffs on 5th December 1922. There were 78 people committed for trial and sentencing that day. Five charges were brought against Edith Thompson. She was charged with the wilful murder of Percy Thompson, conspiring with Bywaters to murder Thompson, administering poison to the victim with intent to murder him, with soliciting and inciting Bywaters to murder Thompson, and with soliciting and inciting Bywaters to conspire with her to murder Thompson.

The Recorder, Sir Ernest Wild, KC, in addressing the Grand Jury, referred to the Ilford murder and recalled in detail the evidence given at the police court, which, he said, indicated that Bywaters and Mrs Thompson had been for some time, "on the most affectionate terms". He said that the correspondence which had passed between them would throw a considerable light on the charges against the woman. In addition to the expressions of affection there were a number of passages which, it was alleged, showed that, for a long time, Thompson had discussed with Bywaters the possibility of killing her husband, and that she even suggested methods, such as the administration of poison or powdered glass. He also stated that from some of the passages in the correspondence it appeared that she had actually attempted to "bring about his death" and that in many of the letters she discussed the question of what the couple should do together when they had succeeded in killing Percy Thompson. The newspaper stated: "Therefore, it would be perfectly clear, the Recorder thought, that there was abundant evidence to justify the Grand Jury in finding a true bill, not only against Bywaters, but against Mrs Thompson on all charges."

The Crown's case was that Thompson was the dominant partner. The trial opened on 6th December 1922 and large crowds – including many women – besieged the Old Bailey. Thompson was frequently in tears as the trial began, but was prevented from collapsing by water and smelling salts. Interestingly, for the first time in a murder trial, a woman, who was "locked up" with a female bailiff until the trial began, was selected to the jury. Good-looking Bywaters was the first to enter the dock. Two minutes later, Thompson walked slowly across the court to join him. Both pleaded not guilty and the case was opened by a long legal argument on an application by Whiteley and Bennett that letters written by Thompson to Bywaters should not be read. However, Justice Sherman ruled that they were admissible as evidence of intention and motive. Inskip then opened the prosecution for the Crown. When the case for the prosecution ended on 7th December, Bywaters took the stand to tell his story. He told how he'd managed to persuade Percy Thompson to begin treating his wife properly and promised him that he would no longer "knock her about", and that Mrs Thompson had persuaded him that they should have a pact to commit suicide should anything go wrong in their relationship. He also said that he never believed that the accused had tried to murder her husband with poison. However, while the Thompsons had discussed separation and divorce, Percy would not agree to either.

On 8th December, Edith Thompson told the court her version of events, when called as a witness in the case against Bywaters.

She denied that she had ever attempted to kill her husband, either by poison or ground glass. The first two years of marriage, she stated, had been happy, but after that things had deteriorated. There were troubles and tensions which led to some inappropriate behaviour from Percy Thompson, including him striking her and throwing her across a room. She remained quiet and pale throughout her own cross-examination by the prosecution. While Bywaters told the court that he agreed to help Thompson with whatever she wanted with regard to her husband in order to keep her calm, the co-accused clearly gave the impression that she had wanted to do whatever he wanted in order to retain his love. In an impassioned appeal to the jury, Sir Curtis Bennett, who had not finished speaking when the court adjourned, argued that every action of Mrs Thompson's on the night of the murder showed that she knew nothing of what was going to happen. He said: "This woman is one of the most extraordinary personalities you or I have ever met. Bywaters described her truly, did he not, when he said she was a woman who lived in melodrama. She was a woman who lived an extraordinary life of make-believe. Have you ever read letters mixed up with criticisms of books and the most beautiful language of love? Whatever name was given to it, it was certainly a great love that existed between the two people." He stated: "They agreed to wait five years for each other. Was that an arrangement of murderers?" He continued that the letters were "the outpouring of a hysterical melodramatic brain". In an appeal for Bywaters, his defence claimed that he was "weak, but no murderer". Whiteley said that in order to convict Bywaters of murder the prosecution had to satisfy them that when the blow was struck, Bywaters had the intent to kill Thompson, and that there was an intent preceding the act. "The tragedy in this case," said counsel gravely, "the poignant tragedy so far as Bywaters is concerned, is that there is sitting next to him in that dock one who is charged jointly with him, one who is dearer to him than his own life." He continued: "If you come to the conclusion Bywaters did not start the fight with the intention of using his knife, and that he used it in the heat of passion in consequence of an attack made on him by Thompson, you are entitled to reduce this crime from murder to manslaughter. Or, again, if you are satisfied Thompson struck him a blow on the chest, followed by the words, 'I will shoot you', and there would be such provocation as will enable you to reduce the crime from murder to manslaughter." During the inquest it transpired that Bywaters had pushed Edith Thompson aside and hustled her husband down the street so that he could have a "word" with the victim. However, it was alleged that Thompson had started a fight with Bywaters and threatened to kill him. After a five-day trial, Edith Jessie Thompson and Frederick Edward Francis Bywaters were found guilty of murdering Percy Thompson. They were both sentenced to death.

The jury took just two and a half hours to find both the accused guilty of murder and Thompson began sobbing, pleading her innocence before she collapsed on hearing the verdicts. Bywaters even pleaded to the court that Thompson was in no way guilty. As

Thompson was led from court she was heard to utter: "Not guilty. Oh, God, not guilty."

Edith Thompson's appeal was to be lodged on 15th December 1922, and Freddie Bywaters was reported to be going to appeal also. Thompson was held in Holloway, while her lover was incarcerated in Pentonville. During the same period, Daisy Wright, who was also sentenced to death for murdering her two-year-old daughter by throwing her into the Thames at Tower Bridge, received a reprieve. Both Ilford murder appeals, however, were dismissed, as it was decided that Edith's letters were "ample proof of guilt". A day of legal arguments on 21st December saw the Lord Chief Justice observe that in a crime which had no redeeming feature, the victim, Percy Thompson, was the only person who excited sympathy. Meanwhile, the Home Secretary granted a reprieve to Ellen Jones for the murder of Florence Stevens, as well as three men. But, in the Thompson appeal, the letters were described as "venomous".

On 6th January 1923, it was announced that the Home Secretary would not intervene in the cases, and the doomed lovers' executions would be carried out as planned. Mr W C Bridgeman refused a reprieve for either of the convicted killers and the official statement read: "The Secretary of State, after careful consideration of all the circumstances, is unable to advise interference with the due course of the law in the cases of Frederick Edward Francis Bywaters and Edith Jessie Thompson, who were convicted of the murder of Percy Thompson." Edith was the first woman to be hanged in more than 15 years in Britain. Her execution was to follow that of Rhoda Willis, a baby farmer and murderer who had been hanged in Cardiff in August 1907.

On 9th January, both Edith Thompson and Freddie Bywaters faced the scaffold. The executions took place at Holloway and Pentonville, respectively, at 9.00am. After a night of semi-consciousness, with a doctor in constant attendance, Thompson was dazed but able, with assistance, to walk to the scaffold, according to the newspaper reports at the time. However, 33 years after Thompson's execution, Home Secretary Major Lloyd George was forced to dismiss allegations that she had fought and struggled with warders prior to her death. He said: "Before the execution the Governor of Holloway prison, who was also the medical officer, gave Mrs Thompson sedatives. The Governor considered that it would be more humane to spare her the necessity of walking the few yards to the execution chamber. Although he thought that she could have walked with assistance, he had her carried and she was supported on the scaffold. Apart from this, nothing unusual happened. Having examined all the information available, I am satisfied that there is no truth in the allegation that Mrs Thompson 'disintegrated as a human creature' or that she 'fought, kicked, screamed and protested her innocence to the last' or that 'it required about five men to hold her down whilst being carried to the gallows and having the noose put over her'." During her last hours, she frequently inquired after Bywaters. He was calm to the end. He smoked a final cigarette a few moments before the death sentence was carried out, and walked firmly from his cell.

Outside Holloway prison, a crowd began gathering at around 9.00am. One woman carried a banner that said: "Murder cannot be abolished by murder." The under sheriff of Essex, Hamilton Gepp, arrived at the prison soon after 8.00am and was joined by the prison chaplain. The official notice of Thompson's execution was posted at 9.33am – it read: "We, the undersigned, hereby declare that the judgment of death was this day executed on Edith J Thompson in his Majesty's prison at Holloway. Hamilton Gepp, Under Sheriff G Murray, Chaplain J H Morton, Governor." Mr Ellis was the executioner, who was assisted by his junior, Albert Pierrepoint, a man who would become the main executioner in Britain over subsequent decades. No black flag was hoisted and no bell tolled.

Winnie Ruth Judd

1931

There was uproar in Hollywood in 1931 when the bodies of two young women were found in two trunks. According to Reuters, the trickle of blood through the trunk made a baggage agent curious and led to a "most gruesome" mystery. The two trunks had just arrived at the Southern Pacific terminus in Los Angeles when the bodies were discovered. The man and woman who had turned up to collect the baggage then mysteriously disappeared. When the trunks were finally opened by officials they were found to contain the mutilated and dismembered bodies of two women. One of the women was described as around 30 years old with black hair, while the other was a woman in her twenties with red hair. The younger woman had been shot. Police tentatively identified the dead women as Mrs Agnes LeRoi, an X-ray technician at the Grunow Memorial Clinic from Phoenix, Arizona – from where the trunks had come – and Hedvig Samuelson, her housemate. As a result of police inquiries, a warrant was issued for the arrest of Winnie (known as Ruth, her middle name) Judd, a secretary at a nursing clinic in Phoenix for first-degree murder.

The doctor's wife and minister's daughter was blasted all over the newspapers and her photo published in October 1931, cabled from New York by the *Mirror*'s Bartlane process, Western Union transmission. An arrest was expected imminently after the police released a woman broadly answering the description of Mrs Judd. However, the motive behind the crimes was still a mystery. Police were inclined to believe that the murderer possessed a "deranged mind". Officials in Los Angeles had refused to hand over the trunks to the man and woman who had appeared to collect them and then promptly disappeared – there was still no trace of the woman, whom police desperately wanted to interview. However, they had traced the man – Mr B J McKinnell, a Los Angeles university student, who turned out to be Judd's brother. He admitted to police that he went to the station to collect the trunks with his sister, but denied all knowledge as to whether she had killed the women suspected to be her colleagues at the nursing home. But, in an interview with an Associated Press staff member, he was alleged to have said that his sister had confessed to the killing of her two companions. Meanwhile, Dr Judd, Ruth's husband, was questioned at length by police and stated that he knew nothing of the crimes.

Ruth Judd stood trial on 19th January 1932 for the murder of both victims. Her lawyers intimated that she would plead not guilty and set up a plea of insanity. Both women were killed at the bungalow in which they lived. According to reports, a "furious quarrel" had broken out at the home, which led to blows. Judd claimed that in a struggle for a revolver, she had shot both women. She was alleged to have packed both bodies into trunks, which she later removed to her own home before consigning them by rail to Los Angeles. Judd had finally surrendered to police four days after the warrant was released for her arrest. Thousands of people flooded Phoenix for the start of the trial.

A verdict of murder in the first degree, which automatically carried the death penalty, was returned on 9th February 1932 for the woman dubbed "Tigress Judd". The 27-year-old showed remarkable calm as the verdict was read out. Throughout the three-week trial she had remained composed: the only evidence of her nervousness was the winding of a handkerchief around her left hand. After the verdict she walked out of the court without making a sound, and, on reaching her cell, she looked at herself in the mirror for a considerable time. Her counsel had pleaded that she was insane, having been threatened with the gun by one of the dead women before she shot them both, but the jury and judge decided otherwise and Judd's execution by hanging was due to take place on 23rd February.

Judd was supported throughout her trial for the murders of her colleague and the young schoolteacher who was undergoing treatment at the clinic at the time by her husband. He was in court to hear how his wife had mutilated the bodies before packing them in trunks and sending them by train to LA. Judd alleged that the schoolteacher had threatened her with the gun, so she wrestled it from her before the shooting began. While Judd was incarcerated awaiting her execution, her lawyers were said to be launching an appeal. They had argued in court that the defendant should be sent to an asylum. On 1st April 1933, the death sentence was confirmed by the Arizona Board of Pardons and Paroles. Judd was granted a reprieve for a short time, but the Supreme Court rejected her appeal. The Phoenix Grand Jury had recommended that the sentence should be commuted to life imprisonment but that was also rejected. However, a stay of execution of the sentence of death was demanded by the state warden just over two weeks later, pending an inquiry into Judd's mental condition. The warden was of the opinion that the woman had become insane. Three days after Judd should have faced the gallows on 21st April 1933, the court judged the murderer to be "insane", and the death sentence was automatically suspended. It was reported by Reuters that the woman would spend the rest of her life in a "lunatic asylum". This brought to an end to one of the most sensational legal "dramas" that the United States had ever seen. Headed by Paul W Schenck, a well-known Hollywood lawyer, the defence team had fought hard to save the killer's life. Three times Judd was reprieved while investigations as to her mental state were carried out by the Arizona State authorities. There was some controversy over the case when, in court, Judd claimed that her illicit affair with a man named Jack Halloran had caused growing tension between her and the two women over his affections, culminating in the murders. The case against Halloran – who was alleged to have taken part in the murders – was thrown out by the judge who found the state's case inconsistent. Despite Judd's testimony implication that he was also responsible, Halloran was never called to court.

After escaping from Arizona State Hospital in Phoenix six times, Judd escaped one last time in October 1963. She ended up in San Francisco Bay where she became a live-in maid for a wealthy family, before she was recaptured in 1969. After two years of legal wrangling for her release, Judd was finally freed in 1971. She died in 1998, at the age of 93, exactly 67 years after her surrender to police.

Women Killers

Gertrude De La Mare

1935

Two Scotland Yard officers were called in to assist the Island Police and were present in Guernsey Court on 8th February 1935 when the inquest opened on Alfred Brouard, 76, a farmer from St Andrews who had been found dead with knife wounds just a few days before. Police Inspector Sculpher said at the inquest that Mr Brouard had been found in bed shortly before 8.00am on the Wednesday he died. The previous evening he'd sat with Mrs De La Mare, his housekeeper, in the sitting room, before she retired to bed at around 9.20pm. He wasn't seen again until he was found dead the following morning. A letter marked for the attention of the police was found in his bedroom and handed to the coroner, Mr H J Casey. Mrs De La Mare was charged in the police court of altering the victim's will and was remanded for a week; meanwhile, the inquest was adjourned.

Later that same month, the newspapers were asking whether the elderly farmer was left or right handed. The issue was raised by the eminent Scotland Yard pathologist, Sir Bernard Spilsbury, who reached Guernsey by boat on 11th February 1935. The dead man had been found with his right arm doubled under him, and as the wound from which he died was inflicted with great force with a blunt knife, the pathologist deemed the question of vital importance. For three hours the same day he arrived, Sir Bernard conducted a post-mortem examination in the mortuary. He was expected to give preliminary medical evidence the following day at the inquest, which was to be reopened. Earlier on 11th February, Sir Bernard had accompanied Chief Inspector Duncan and Sergeant Smart from Scotland Yard to the house in St Andrews where the murder victim had lived. They remained there for about half an hour while a reconstruction was staged and a number of measurements were taken. The senior police officers and pathologist then held a meeting with Inspector Sculpher of the Island Police. It also transpired that De La Mare's husband attended the police station for 45 minutes before leaving for a neighbour's house where his daughter, aged two, was staying, before returning to the Cobo district where he lived. Twenty-seven-year-old Mrs De La Mare was, meanwhile, still on remand for forging the will, after her application for bail failed.

By 12th February it was known that Sir Bernard did not believe the farmer to have committed suicide. He told the inquest: "In my opinion, the wound was not self-inflicted." Sir Bernard had spent some considerable time examining the body, and later Camp Joinet Farm in St Andrews. The imposing white-stone building was hidden from the road by trees and screened at the back and side by a high granite wall. Before Brouard took up farming he had been a schoolteacher in St Martins. He was a well-known resident of Guernsey and one of its oldest at the time of his death. He was described as a cheerful man, who was well liked. Gertrude De La

Mare had entered service as his housekeeper two and half years prior to the murder; she lived at the farmhouse with her daughter after separating from her husband. There were rumours as the inquest reopened that the police were digging in the back garden of the property.

Discoveries made by police investigating the death confirmed their suspicions of foul play on 13th February, and a charge of murder was considered. However, Inspector Sculpher refused to divulge any information to the press or public. Police did, however, confirm that the murder weapon was not dropped by the victim in the spot where it was found by Sergeant Le Lievre of the Island Police. The victim's bedroom at the farm was the smallest room in the house and was favoured by him for sentimental reasons. He had been born in the house and had lived there all his life. The bedroom was where he preferred to spend his time, with its little window overlooking the front door. While police denied they were "digging" in the back garden, they did confirm that they had been searching a pile of rubbish at the rear of the premises, which included a quantity of bedding that had been taken from the bed where the dead man had been found. The bedding had been partially burned and the charred remains were carefully examined by detectives in the hope of finding a clue. The question being asked across Guernsey was whether the victim had been drugged prior to his death. It was a line of inquiry being followed up in the search for the murderer, and Sir Bernard had taken certain organs of the victim back to London for special analysis. Brouard's funeral took place on 13th February, attended by scores of islanders. Meanwhile, microscope tests were carried out on a bloodstained handkerchief found near the home of the victim. It had initials worked into one corner in red cotton and had been found caught in barbed wire surrounding the garden of the farmhouse.

A sensational development in the case came on Saturday 23rd February when it was announced that Gertrude De La Mare had been charged with murdering her employer and taken to court. She appeared on remand, charged with forging and issuing a document purporting to be Brouard's will, and when the new charge was read her hands clenched tightly on the wooden partition in front of the dock. She said: "My Lord, God is above me, and He knows what I am saying. I am not guilty of murder, nor of the document that I am charged with." After her plea, the court was cleared of the public and, in accordance with Guernsey procedure, the hearing took place in camera. Despite heavy rain, crowds of people, mostly women, waited outside for hours before the court opened. Chief Inspector Duncan carried a number of exhibits into court, including a piece of brown carpet, which he carefully placed on the floor. De La Mare showed great emotion as she stood in the dock. Four witnesses were called including Duncan, Sculpher, Le Lievre and a man named Cachon, who held a position equivalent with assistant borough surveyor. It was the first time in the history of the island court that a woman had been charged with murder. It was also the first time for a century in which the island court had seen a murder trial. During the "hearing in camera", 33 witnesses had been called. It was then announced that all 33, plus three new witnesses, would be called to the actual trial. The Prime Minister of Guernsey, Mr A W Bell, was to take the role of presiding judge. Just a few days before, he had sat on the bench as bailiff of the island during an historic session of Guernsey's Parliament, in which the question of divorce law for the island had been debated.

Gertrude Elizabeth De La Mare had spent her days on remand writing, setting down her thoughts, and had covered scores of sheets of foolscap in scriptural language. She had attended the prison church service each week, and things remained quiet; however, the drama became tense and harrowing towards the end of the first day of the trial. For two hours the Attorney General had addressed the court, before senior police officers were questioned for a further two hours. Next De La Mare took the stand, but proceedings were adjourned as the bailiff and jury were taken to visit the farmhouse where the murder took place. The prisoner was taken too and all watched as a reconstruction of the crime was staged. Hanging in the greenhouse and stretching through the garden into the kitchen was a line of bloodstained blankets and sheets, each a numbered exhibit. De La Mare was escorted from the back of the property, through the garden, past the gruesome reminders of murder, into the house and up to the tiny bedroom. While the prosecution stated how she had committed the crime, the accused was allowed to argue her case and show the judge and jury how she had found the dead man before fleeing to a neighbour for help. The drama increased when a police officer lay on the bed in the same position as the victim had been in when he was found. The day had been a grim ordeal for all involved, and De La Mare was visibly shaken as she was returned to prison. The opening of the trial was much lighter than the events that ended day one, and after the Lord's Prayer had been read by the clerk in French, Mr Bell began proceedings in his customary gentle manner. Even the warders guarding De La Mare whispered to the accused and encouraged her with smiles. However, it transpired that bloodstained garments had been found in the home of a lady named Mrs Thomas – a friend of the accused – and given to police. Speaking for the defence, the counsel, Randell, said: "He is no more qualified than would be a medicine man or a witch doctor", when giving the Royal Court his thoughts on Sir Bernard and his examinations. The eminent pathologist and Dr Roche Lynch, the Home Office analyst, had arrived in Guernsey to give their findings in the case, but Mr H Randell objected to any evidence from Spilsbury on the grounds that he had not been admitted to medical practice on the island. "It would be just as right to bring a man from the most uncivilised country in the world to give evidence as it would be to call Sir Bernard, who, as far as Guernsey is concerned, is not a qualified medical man," he said. "We have a rule that nobody may act as a doctor unless he had been admitted to practice here. However much faith we may have in Sir Bernard – and I myself do not wish to disparage in any way his qualifications – he is not a qualified man as far as Guernsey is concerned." However, the judge thought that the court should have the best evidence available at its disposal and overruled the objection. Sir Bernard said that from its extent, the depth and wound in Brouard's throat was "of a determined character" and he was of the opinion that the wound could not have been self-inflicted with the weapon (a bread knife known to belong to De La Mare).

Mr Randell, undeterred by the overruled objection, asked Lemasurier, manager of the Guernsey branch of Midland Bank: "Do you think Mr Brouard had a hold over Mrs De La Mare over some financial matters?" "Yes," came the reply from the bank manager. On 6th April 1935, De La Mare's mother was called into court to give evidence for the prosecution against her daughter. She said: "My daughter was employed by Mr Brouard for only 8s. a week. She worked very hard and she certainly did not get much good food ... I always saw that he was a very rough man ... I told him once that it would be better for my daughter if she left his place and went somewhere she could earn more money for herself and her daughter, but he did not want to let my daughter go." Asked if she had seen her daughter prior to the murder the witness nodded and said: "Three days before. She told me she had found Mr Brouard with his throat cut. I said: 'Surely Gertie, you are mad.'" There was an audible "ripple" across the courtroom and mother's and daughter's eyes met. Under cross-examination by Mr Randell, the accused's mother confirmed that her daughter had not left the employ of Brouard because she owed him some money. The judge then asked defence counsel if they would be pleading insanity, to which the answer was: "Yes".

On 9th April 1935, De La Mare fought a "duel" for her life, for four hours with the island's Attorney General. Hour after hour questions were put to the defendant. The Attorney General was sudden, devastating and vehement in his approach, but to each and every question the young woman answered in the negative. She told him: "I am here between life and death." The matter then turned to the suggestion that an intruder had killed the farmer. One doctor, however, suggested that De La Mare was suffering from "madness" and that she couldn't possibly say she killed the farmer because: "She doesn't know if she did." Dr W McGlashan, superintendent of the mental hospital on the island, said: "I think Mrs De La Mare is a lunatic, a moral defective, suffering from minor epilepsy … with 68 per cent of the mentality of a child of eleven." Even the Attorney General was taken aback. He continued: "I believe that on that Sunday, when she told her mother that Mr Brouard had cut his throat, she had hallucinations. Her life for the next two days indicates return to sanity. I think it possible that on Wednesday (the day of Brouard's death), she had a complete fit of petit mal." Carefully choosing his words, the doctor continued: "If she did cut the throat … I am confident it was done during an epileptic equivalent, and that she has no memory of having committed the act." However, the prison doctor, Dr Carey, did not agree that the defendant was "insane" and dismissed the suggestion of petit mal.

The defendant's mother, Mrs Victorine Marie Yvonne le Page, was recalled to the witness box by the prosecution to give evidence, while Randell submitted that the accused could not be convicted because of a flaw in the indictment. On 13th April the newspapers stated that the case had been "bungled" from the start. Counsel for De La Mare suggested once again that the farmer had been killed by an unknown assailant, who could have got into the unlocked house the night before the killing. He also accused the police and doctors involved of "bungling" the entire case. However, any pleas of insanity were strongly contested by the Attorney General, Mr A J Sherwill, when he made his final speech for the Crown. He also described the accused as "an appalling liar". He said: "That the prisoner with her own hand killed Mr Brouard cold-bloodedly … If I am right, she is either a dastardly murderess or else she is a dangerous lunatic." He continued: "The prosecution do not suggest that the prisoner is wholly normal; on the contrary, it appears that she is not, but between abnormality of behaviour and insanity to the point of making her criminally irresponsible a great gulf exists."

On 16th April, Gertrude De La Mare was found guilty by just one jurat (judges of fact rather than law in Guernsey and Jersey), and sentenced to death on the scaffold. She remained calm and composed as Randell told the *Mirror*: "She was as calm and as unconcerned as she had been all through the trial. She spoke of a man being involved, which information I passed on to the police. In Guernsey law there is no appeal against the sentence. I can do nothing more than send all the papers of the case to the Home Secretary and ask for the King's clemency." If there was no reprieve, a scaffold would have to be built and a hangman sent from England as well as a special law passed to prohibit public executions – which were, at the time, allowed under Guernsey's law. The 11 jurats had filed back into court. The death penalty was decided by six votes to five. As the bailiff donned his black bonnet the defendant said: "The only thing I have to say is that I know I have not done it. That is the only true thing. God is above me. The Attorney General has been against me for that, but God knows I have not done it. I am quite prepared to face death because I know I have not done it." It was the first time that the death penalty had ever been passed on a woman in the history of Guernsey's legal proceedings.

In May 1935, a full report of the case was sent to the Home Office for consideration, but it would be some time before it was known if the King would grant clemency.

On 15th May, it was reported that three women throughout Britain waited in suspense to hear their fates. It was then stated that one would have her life spared. The other two were set to be executed as sentenced. Gertrude De La Mare was the one woman who received a reprieve. Her sentence had been commuted to life imprisonment. The convicted murderer was said to be "overjoyed" at the news, broken to her by the sheriff of the island and the prison governor. She was then taken to a women's prison in England. The other women, two sisters, Rose Edwards and Elizabeth Edwards, who had both been found guilty of the murder of the latter's illegitimate child, had their appeal against their sentence dismissed by the Irish Free State Court of Criminal Appeal. The body of the child was never found, but the court held that the jury was entitled to infer that it died a violent death at the hands of the accused. Both sisters were to be executed on 31st May 1935.

On the grounds that his wife had a commuted death sentence, Gertrude's husband was granted a divorce. The decree was granted in Guernsey's Court of Matrimonial Causes in June 1947.

Charlotte Bryant

1936

In January 1936, police guarded a dead man's cottage, which stood on the slopes of a lonely valley and could only be reached by a cart track, waiting for the arrival of Scotland Yard detectives to begin investigations. All visitors had been turned away, and relatives were instructed to make no statements. The whole affair, in fact, seemed to be shrouded in mystery. Frederick John Bryant, 39, a cowman, lived with his wife and five children in the little hamlet of Coombe, two miles from Sherborne in Dorset. For the previous two years, Bryant had been employed by a farmer in the neighbourhood, but two weeks before Christmas 1935 he had been taken ill. On 22nd December he was admitted to the Yeatman Hospital in Sherborne, where he died. When the inquest was opened on Christmas Eve no members of the public or press were present and the only evidence of identity was given by the man's widow. Some of the man's organs, fingernails and hair were sent to London for examination, and as a result of a preliminary report Chief Inspector Bell of Scotland Yard and another officer were sent to Sherborne. Bryant's wife was interviewed by police for some time on 1st January, and their children were taken away from the family home in an unknown vehicle.

The purchase of arsenic from a local chemist and the torn fragments of a letter, in the possession of police, were regarded as important clues. Charlotte Bryant, 36, and the five children, whose ages ranged from 13 years to 12 months, were rehomed in Sturminster Institution, while Bell and Detective Sergeant Tapsell took yet another statement from the widowed woman. Bryant's sister told reporters that her brother had been ill three times since May 1935, while other detectives searched a brook which ran close to the farm where the dead man worked. As Frederick Bryant was suspected to have died from arsenic poisoning, all the family pets, including a terrier dog, a cat, and some pigeons and poultry, at the house where the family lived were killed and taken away for scientific examination. The killing of the animals was carried out by an RSPCA official from Yeovil. Meanwhile, further searches of the cottage were undertaken and bundles of clothing, including a man's suit, were taken away. A local photographer, instructed by police, took photographs of parts of the garden and the inside of the house, and police began digging in the garden. Poisons registers were also being checked by police in Dorset, Somerset and other neighbouring counties, while the authorities were anxious to trace a family friend who had recently stayed at the cottage.

Investigations into the poison riddle were renewed on 10th February and an arrest was expected imminently. Five weeks of investigating had been undertaken as to why the cowman had died in agony within an hour of his arrival in hospital, just before Christmas. It then transpired that Charlotte Bryant had said: "I think before long I shall be a widow. Will you marry me then?" She was accused of uttering those words to the family lodger; this was brought up at an inquest in late February 1936, where she stood accused of murdering her husband. "There is plenty of evidence to show that she preferred the lodger to her husband," said counsel. He added that Charlotte Bryant was said to have asked a friend: "What would you give to anyone if you wanted to get rid of them?" The children remained in the workhouse as their mother faced the inquest for murder. Opening the inquest, Mr H Parham described how Bryant was taken ill and was unwilling to go to hospital. His employer arranged for Lucy Ostler, a friend of the accused, to stay in the cottage and look after him, but after being relieved of her duties at 3.00am by Charlotte Bryant, she heard the accused say: "Will you have the Oxo, Fred? I have just put the hot water on it." Fred Bryant agreed, but soon after was heard vomiting by Lucy. The following morning he was in a very bad state and unable to get out of bed. Dr Roche Lynch, also instrumental in the Gertrude De La Mare case, found four grains of arsenious oxide in Bryant's organs. It was clear that he had received a large dose – it was cited that two grains would be fatal. After the police had taken medicine from the cottage, Mrs Bryant told her son to clear out some bottles and tins, and took a tin from a cupboard, which contained paraffin, and on which was written, "Weed Killer – Poison". She told her son that she had to get rid of the bottles and tins and that she was going to burn rubbish in the copper fire, but it would not draw. One of the tins was later thrown on a rubbish heap in the garden and police found that it contained 5.8 per cent of arsenious oxide. Parham then told the inquest of an earlier conversation between

Bryant and Ostler where the former had asked her friend what she was reading in a Sunday newspaper. Bryant, was interested in the poison case that Ostler was studying. The motive that the prosecutor gave the inquest was that for more than two years Bryant had been "on terms of greatest intimacy with Leonard Parsons", the family's lodger. She had also quite openly said that Parsons was the father of her youngest child. Bryant's employer, farmer Aubrey Robert Priddle, was called to court to give evidence and told the inquest how he had visited his dying employee and had "words" with the man's wife. The farmer had reprimanded Charlotte Bryant for going out and leaving her husband at home in agony. Twice he had called to see his employee and twice he found him alone, suffering in agony. Another witness, Ellen Stone, told the inquest how she had visited Fred Bryant and also found him alone. She said: "Bryant told me that he had burning pains in his inside, and that he was poisoned and was dying." In mid-March, Mrs Bryant was given permission to see her children. She was then remanded in Holloway prison in London before she faced a trial at Dorchester Assizes. One of the last acts she did before making her way to the dock was to send a letter to her five children. She told them that they would not see her for some time, until she "got out of her present trouble". The letter, written in childish handwriting, was addressed to Ernest and Lily, her eldest children. The first day of the trial, which began on 28th May, involved the dead man's mother and Lucy Ostler. While the prosecution witnesses gave evidence, the defendant sat with red eyes, fumbling nervously with a handkerchief. Under cross-examination Lucy Ostler had to admit that no one else apparently saw the tin which she had willingly brought to the attention of police. She was also questioned over her own husband's death four years earlier. Furthermore, the defence brought up the fact that it was Lucy Ostler who had been alone with the dead man the night before he died. She even admitted that she had been afraid when she made her statement to police – the defence counsel suggested that was because the police could easily have suspected her, and not Charlotte Bryant.

Lily Bryant, aged 10, was called to court to give evidence. At the sight of her daughter, Charlotte Bryant burst into tears. Composed and serious, Lily told Mr J D Caswell, her mother's counsel, what had happened at home just prior to her father's death. She told the court how she had lit a fire beneath the copper but had found no tin in the pile of rubbish left for burning. She also told the court that Leonard Parsons had threatened her mother. Ernest followed his sister into the witness box but did not manage to control his emotions. He began with control while being questioned, but broke down when he spied his mother in tears across the courtroom. Bryant was allowed to see her children following the day's proceedings and all three wept together. Lily Bryant wasn't very well that day and told her mother that for several weeks she had had a temperature, although the doctor had been unable to diagnose any particular complaint. Meanwhile, a large crowd gathered to see the accused woman while Lily was sent to an infirmary. It was reported that Dr Barnardo's Homes had offered to take in the five children from the workhouse.

Later, a letter was sent to the accused. "Dear Mum," it began: "When are you coming back to see us? We all want you back. It has been such a long time sins I had see you. Lily is ill. Please come back soon. From your loving son, Ernest." It was dated 1st June 1936, and brown-eyed Ernest was writing to his mother in Exeter jail, where she was awaiting execution after being convicted of the murder of the children's father, Fred Bryant. A reporter, who travelled to Sturminster in Dorset to see the children, reported that he saw Ernest on the local recreation ground playing cricket with his school friends. "Where is Mum? Is she coming back?" he asked. The reporter had watched the tragic answer to the question, decided by a jury of 12 Dorset men two hours before in the hushed Assizes Court in Dorchester. Charlotte Bryant had been half-carried from the dock after the sentence of death had been passed. He wrote: "I told the boy as gently as possible that the master of Sturminster Institution has something to tell him." "I'm sure she will be back soon," little Ernest told the reporter. "Won't she?" he continued. "I'm sure she will be back," he stated again. The reporter wrote: "It was difficult to look straight at the tearstained little face." George, seven, William, four and a half, and Edwin, 12 months, did not know that their mother was even in prison. Ernest asked the reporter if he thought his mother would be allowed home if he wrote to the judge. There hadn't been a day when Ernest hadn't been in tears. Miles across the sea from the tragic children, in Londonderry, the convicted woman's mother and two sisters wept at Charlotte's fate. By the end of June 1936, her appeal against the death sentence had been dismissed in the Law Courts, and she had already written to her children to tell them she would never see them again. "Think of me as I last was," she wrote in a letter from Exeter jail to Ernest, before she left for Holloway prison and the Court of Criminal Appeal. In the tearstained note, the condemned mother asked him to let his brothers and sister know that she was thinking of them always. However, there was a possibility that the case might be brought up in the House of Lords. Some medical evidence had been admitted to court which had been unobtainable at the trial. Mr J G Grapnell, KC, for Mrs Bryant said: "It has come to the knowledge of the defence that Professor William Bone of the Imperial College of Science, has volunteered information that there has been a grave mistake regarding the quantum of arsenic normally found in ash of coal." Lord Hewart, however, after consulting with his colleagues on the bench, said sternly: "The Court is unanimously of opinion that there is no occasion for the further evidence." He continued: "If this Court, on the conclusion of a capital charge or other case were to listen to the after thoughts of a scientific gentleman who brought his mind controversially to bear on evidence that has been given, it would be intolerable."

The following month, the five children arrived in Liverpool, bound for Ireland where they were to live with their grandmother. That same month, on 7th July, Charlotte Bryant's final appeal failed and her plea for the case to go before the House of Lords was refused. On 13th July, just three days before her execution was due to be carried out, she made a last dramatic bid for life by writing to the Home Secretary, Sir John Simon, begging for a reprieve. Questions concerning the refusal of the Court of Criminal Appeal to admit new evidence were to be put to the Solicitor General in the House of Commons the following day. It was reported that all the condemned woman's thoughts were for her children. Her solicitor, Christopher Arrow, told the *Mirror*: "I was with her for nearly an hour, during which she talked mainly of her children. She was pleased to know they had been moved from the institution to the home of a friend and begged that they should never know what had happened to her if she dies on Wednesday. She has been through so much during the past few months that she seems resigned to whatever her fate is to be, though she protests her innocence time and again." Despite her plea to the Home Secretary, Simon told Sir Stafford Cripps, KC, that he saw no grounds for interfering in the case. Sir Stafford had approached him on the convicted woman's behalf, appealing for a new trial and the need to call fresh evidence.

In December 1961, housewife Lilian Scarrott said: "It is terrible to think that my mother may have been hanged because of a mistake. But it is wonderful to think that perhaps now people will stop hounding and shaming me because I am my mother's daughter." It was 25 years since Charlotte Bryant had faced the gallows for the crime of murdering Lilian's father. But, in a book published on 4th December 1961, author Casswell said that new evidence could have cleared her of the murder. After the death sentence was passed, the new evidence was refused admittance by Hewart. A senior analyst at the Home Office told the court that the amount of arsenic in the ashes where the charred tin – the only real evidence – was found was abnormally high. However, Professor Bone proved that the analyst had made a "terrible blunder". He had been given the result over the phone and it is believed that he misheard what was actually relayed to him.

Lilian Scarrott revealed all those years later how she and her brothers were separated after the trial. They hadn't set sail for Ireland and the comfort of being with their grandmother after all, but had been placed in an orphanage before they were sent to different foster homes. "We wrote a little, then decided to stay apart as the shame of being the children of a murderess was too much. But, people found out who my mother was and abused me. Sometimes women spat at me in the street. I have changed my address 11 times trying to start afresh. Often I have lain awake at night wondering how my brothers fared. Now I hope they may get in touch for a family reunion." Mrs Scarrott took the hand of her husband and said: "Now I feel that the children of Charlotte Bryant will find happiness."

Carmen Swann

1936

Valerie Swann, aged eight, was found dead in a flat at Clarendon Court, Maida Vale, in West London. Her inquest in Paddington, held on 14th February 1936, heard evidence that the little girl's father had committed suicide on her birthday. George Vasilesco, the child's maternal uncle, said that his sister had married an Englishman called Leonard Clarkson Swann, a bank clerk, in 1923. Swann was known to have been an in-patient at a local hospital for nervous diseases and had had to give up his work, so his wife returned to her profession as a secretary. She was known to have suffered from depression. Dr John Baldie, who was called to the flat, said that he found the child dead in one bed, and a woman unconscious in another. There was a tumbler beside one of the beds with a small amount of crystallized sediment in the bottom, a cup containing tea, some sweets and some phials. The tap of a gas fire was partly turned on, but there was no gas escaping. Sir Bernard Spilsbury said that at his first examination he could see no definite cause of the child's death. She had been perfectly healthy. Carmen Swann, Valerie's mother, was found guilty of her murder and sentenced to death, but within 24 hours she was reprieved. Her spared life, however, would mean a "living death" for the murderer who was already dying. Six months prior to the murder of her daughter, Swann had been told that she was dying of tuberculosis by doctors. The reprieve, granted on 26th March 1936, was one of the swiftest ever by a Home Secretary. It followed a grim trial at the Old Bailey where the bitter tragedy unfolded.

Swann, 32, had discovered four months after her marriage that her mother-in-law was living in a "mental" home. When Valerie was born, Swann's husband had already been declared insane. On the child's fourth birthday, he hung himself, and Carmen Swann discovered his body. She then found out that she only had a slim chance of recovering from tuberculosis, while Valerie developed bronchitis. By the time of Valerie's death, Swann was convinced that the child had caught tuberculosis and was suffering insanity inherited from her father's side. Mother and daughter had decided to die together, but Swann survived the suicide pact. As a result of the Home Secretary's decision to reprieve the woman from execution, her solicitor fought to ensure her early release from prison so that she could be placed in a sanatorium. He told the *Mirror*: "The trial caused a great stir of public sympathy. I hope to have Mrs Swann moved into a sanatorium, where she can have the best possible treatment. It is too early yet to say if her life can be saved." Carmen Swann left Holloway prison on 29th April 1936, but she didn't pass through the iron-studded doors to freedom as other women prisoners would have done. Instead, she was taken to a London County Council public institution, a destination which was kept a close secret. She died of tuberculosis. Her case was compared to that of Mrs Brownhill who was described as having an "imbecile son", Denis, who, at the age of 30, was completely dependent on his mother. She herself was told by doctors that she needed an emergency operation – which could have proved fatal – so, in anguish, she killed her child.

Josephine Mory
(and Other Murderers)

1937

Josephine Mory, a 47-year-old mother, thought her daughter-in-law wasn't good enough for her son, so she strangled her. Then, to give the appearance of suicide, she hung the woman's body on the back of a door. As the murderer was sentenced to death in Douai, France, on 28th October 1937, spectators in the public gallery, who had been shouting "Give her death", broke into a round of applause. The trial revealed the mother's growing hatred of the woman who had married her son, and the son's battle for happiness with the wife who had been his mistress.

The dead woman, Mlle Yvette, had lived with Mory's son, a lieutenant in the French Army Reserve. They married, despite his parents' opposition, just before the couple had a baby. A second baby was due when the woman was murdered. In court, Mory told of her ambitions for her son, and of her dismay when "he married beneath him". "We made every sacrifice for him," she stated, "... so that he could complete his studies. He should have recompensed us for our sufferings." She had planned for him to marry into a rich, comfortable and respected family. Her husband had even tried to persuade the young woman's uncle and aunt to prevent the marriage. "The girl told me then that she would soon be a mother," he said. "I told her that she could raise the brat herself." The report of a private detective hired by the Morys to investigate the girl's past was also admitted as evidence in court. From statements picked up from people in Rouen, the detective said: "I concluded that this girl was a prostitute, and a private one at that."

The murdered woman's husband, Louis Mory, said that his parents gave him the detective's report, but he immediately checked all the allegations himself and found them to be completely untrue. "My parents continued to complain to me," he said, and continued: "They said, 'This girl is not made for you.'" He explained: "I made numerous visits to conciliate them, but in vain. They had wanted me to make a rich marriage. My mother was continually cursing and threatening me and every time she visited us it was perfect hell." Louis Mory refused to look at his parents during the trial even though his mother called to him and said: "Come, my son, come and kiss me."

This case was followed 11 years later by the riddle of a woman found dead in Lancashire. Nancy Ellen Chadwick, from Rawtenstall, was found dead in a street on 30th August 1948. "We have not yet been able to rule out the possibility of foul play," said a police officer. At the time, almost everyone in the town knew Maggie – the strange, slight little woman dressed in men's clothes – but on 1st September 1948 she caused a "sensation" when she was charged with the murder of Nancy, 70, known as "the woman who loved money". The 42-year-old was arrested by Chief Inspector Bob Stevens after the police paid a 6.00am visit to her house.

Maggie, who lived alone, was an ex-bus conductor and slipper worker who had been out of work since Christmas 1947 following an operation. A friend told the *Mirror*: "We could never discover why she was always dressed as a man. She acted as though it was nothing unusual and never discussed it. In local pubs she was often mistaken for a man by strangers. She spoke in a deep voice with a broad Lancashire accent." Meanwhile, police dragged an electromagnet over the bed of the River Irwell on 2nd September 1948 in a further effort to find the murder weapon. The inquest on Nancy was formally opened the day that Maggie was arrested.

It was alleged that, within an hour and a half of killing Nancy, Maggie went for a drink. Margaret Allen, committed for trial on 23rd September for the murder of the victim, was said to be an eccentric fortune-teller. Nancy had been seen walking towards Allen's home on the morning of her death, but no one saw her again until the headlights of a bus picked out her body lying outside Allen's door at 3.55 the next morning. While out for a drink, Allen was described as "queer" and "giggling". Bloodstains were found at her home by police as well as a damp rag. Nancy Chadwick had been hit over the head up to 10 times or more by something like a hammer. On 9th December, Margaret "Maggie" Allen was sentenced to death at Manchester Assizes for the murder. That same day, Mary Park, and her husband William, were sentenced to death for the murders of their own daughters aged 15, 14 and 12.

At 9.00am on 12th January 1949, Allen was hanged in Manchester's Strangeways jail for her crime. Her friend, Annie

Cook, who stood on the corner of Kay Street and Bacup Road in the city where the condemned woman had asked her to be at the appointed hour, was jeered and mocked by a crowd of angry women, while she cried on the shoulder of her sister, Gladys Flood. Another woman protesting at the hanging was shouted down by the same women.

Louisa Merrifield

1953

It was a quiet Sunday afternoon, and girls in spring dresses passed the green and cream detached bungalow called The Homestead with barely a glance – but behind the heavily curtained windows of the trim dwelling in a "good" suburb, detectives and doctors were investigating a mystery. During the following days, pathologists hoped to be able to give Scotland Yard information, which would help to answer the question as to how Sarah Ann Ricketts had died. Both her husbands had gassed themselves and she trusted no one. At the age of 80, she had no friends and the door of her neat bungalow in Blackpool had barely been opened in 10 years. It was April 1953, and six days earlier she had died at home. Her doctor refused to sign a death certificate. Police cars had travelled daily between Blackpool and Preston in Lancashire taking the dead woman's organs, bed linen and clothing, along with food samples, for examination at police laboratories. Detectives had, meanwhile, been questioning chemists and grocers, and Dr J B Firth, director of the police laboratory, handed a preliminary report to Scotland Yard Superintendent Colin McDougall. Neighbours, it was known, had helped the elderly widow with her shopping. She had lived alone for a long time, but just five weeks earlier she had advertised for a "companion housekeeper", offering a "good home" in return for light duties. As a result, Louisa Merrifield landed the "job", where she hoped to find a comfortable home for herself and her third husband Alfred. She too had lost two husbands.

Merrifield told reporters: "The old lady was mistrustful, suspicious and hard to please. She prepared all her own food, but she preferred drink to food. She would buy a bottle of brandy, a bottle of rum and a case of stout at the same time. I tried to get her to take more nourishing food." She continued: "When we came, Mrs Ricketts was badly neglected. Her legs were swollen and I massaged them for hours. She did not have a lot of money coming in."

On 20th April 1953, two Scotland Yard detectives conferred for 90 minutes with one of Britain's leading forensic science experts in the office of a crime laboratory with regard to the death. The detectives needed to know how the "snappy" and "crotchety" lady died. Her final illness had only lasted a few days and the coroner announced: "This is not a case in which I can issue a cremation order." The woman's daughter, Ethel Harrison, was told only that a burial certificate could be left with police and that the inquest would be adjourned for at least 28 days. Three days later, Louisa Merrifield was taken by police to the police station in Blackpool, where she was accompanied by a solicitor and the coroner's officer. Meanwhile, Sarah Ricketts was buried at Carlton cemetery in a plain, wreathless coffin. Police by now suspected that the woman had been poisoned.

With spades, rakes and a mine detector, three detectives made an inch-by-inch search of the garden and daffodil beds around the victim's bungalow. After two hours searching they left, having politely declined the tea they were offered by Merrifield. She was accused of murdering Sarah Ricketts on 1st May 1953 and remanded at Blackpool. Her 71-year-old husband was in court to see her remanded, but went home to eat a simple meal alone. She made her second appearance in court on 8th May and was told she was still remanded. On 15th May Alfred Merrifield was also arrested on suspicion of murder, as he visited his wife in the cells at Blackpool police station. Two hours later, two police cars pulled up at the murder victim's home and senior detectives entered the living room and closed the heavy curtains. On 20th May, Merrifield handed a handbag to his solicitor; there was a tense 90-minute battle in court before the defence team won the right to keep the handbag and its contents from the police. This began with the Director of Public Prosecution telling the magistrates that he wanted to subpoena the defence lawyer, John Budd, as a witness to produce certain objects. However, under the Common Law rule of privilege, and to protect the relationship between solicitor and client, the objects were declared exempt from being produced in court. Mr Budd said: "If the court holds that these objects must be produced and if it ultimately turns out that they are privileged it may well be that the whole of these proceedings may be vitiated. It may pave the way to the Court of Criminal Appeal and the quashing of any possible conviction."

The Merrifields faced their first full day in court on 27th May 1953. There was "dramatic evidence about a hint of trouble in the camp" at the home the couple shared with the deceased. Sarah Ricketts had died just 14 days after she altered her will, leaving everything to the Merrifields. The penultimate witness, towards the close of the five-hour hearing, Arthur Gardner, a tenant of Mrs Ricketts, entered the box after the Merrifields' solicitor had asked for all other witnesses, except doctors and police, to be sent out of court. The solicitor explained that the evidence from that point on was "likely to be controversial". Gardner described how, on making his fortnightly call at the bungalow to pay his rent, he was met at the door by Mrs Merrifield, who then followed him into the house where he saw the elderly landlady and Mr Merrifield. Gardner thought that Sarah Ricketts was trying to attract his attention. He imagined – he told the court – that she was trying to tell him there was "some trouble in the camp". She pointed at the Merrifields he said, and then shook her head. In court, on either side of the accused couple, sat two warders, a prison officer and a nurse. Several times, Louisa Merrifield looked to be on the point of fainting.

Between 9th and 14th of April, the court heard how Mrs Merrifield had visited three doctors. One she had asked to certify that Sarah had been of sound mind when she rewrote her will, to the second she said that the victim had been seriously ill. That particular doctor had examined Mrs Ricketts and found her fit and well apart from a touch of bronchitis. However, the following day, 14th April, Sarah was examined by a third doctor and found to be dying. Traces of rat poison were found in her system following a post-mortem. In the pathologist's opinion the poison had been administered after 6.30pm on 13th April either in one large dose, or in successive doses through the night. Elisabeth Barrowclough, a witness, then told the court how she had had a conversation at a bus stop with the accused, who had approached her and told how she was "a very worried woman". She said: "She was looking after an old woman who was very ill and she had been to see a solicitor." Louisa Merrifield had told her that when she returned from a visit to Wigan, her husband "was in bed with the old lady", and she heard him say: "Should I massage your legs again, love?" The witness continued: "She said, 'If he does it again I will poison the old ***** and him as well.'" Merrifield was then accused of telling the witness that her husband was greedy and "wants it all his own". Another witness, George Forjan, described how since the Merrifields had lived with Sarah Ricketts her weekly drinks delivery account – consisting of a bottle of rum and bottled stout – had been outstanding, yet prior to this the victim had paid him on delivery each time without fail. He told the court that she complained about the Merrifields and told him that she hadn't eaten properly for three days. The grocery delivery driver reiterated the belief that Sarah wasn't getting enough food as he heard her tell Louisa Merrifield that she wasn't feeding her properly when he called at the house in the days prior to the woman's death. Norah Lowe told the court how she had received a letter from Mrs Merrifield in March, stating that she had been left a bungalow by the old lady that she was looking after, while three days before Sarah Ricketts died another witness, Jessie Brewer, had met the accused in the street and was told the same thing. Both witnesses believed Mrs Ricketts had already died. In fact, Merrifield continually referred to the victim in the past tense, to the point that both women thought Sarah had been dead for some time. When Jessie read in the paper that Sarah died on 14th April, she rang the police to check the date with them, believing that the newspapers had printed it incorrectly. The police promptly went to interview her. Mavis Atkinson, assistant at Cottons Chemists in Manchester, then told the court how Merrifield's husband had bought some Rodine – containing rat poison – from the shop in March. However, Alfred Merrifield exclaimed: "Me! Liar."

As the hearing continued, Esther Fagg, witness for the prosecution, told how she had been present when Mrs Merrifield's friend, Mrs Hands, opened a handbag given to her by the accused containing a spoon that appeared to have a dried substance on it. Hands told her to keep her mouth shut about what she had seen, she told the jury. She also told the court that Merrifield had asked Hands to keep the bag for her should the police start making inquiries. Sir Lionel Heald, QC, the Attorney General prosecuting, told the court in July 1953 that the Merrifields had "an unrivalled opportunity" of killing Sarah. "I might describe it as an exclusive opportunity," he added, "because they were alone in the bungalow with her." He continued that the victim had made a will in "full favour" of the accused husband and wife, but that on the day before she died she obviously had designs to change it back to its original intention.

The all-male jury also heard how bran – one of the main ingredients of rat poison – was found in Sarah's body, yet there was no sign of the tin, and no evidence of the spoon or glass in which the poison was administered. Suicide was not probable, according to the prosecution. Merrifield had further condemned herself by telling one witness, six days before the will was executed and three weeks before Sarah's death, that she had had a bit of luck because the old lady who employed her had left her a bungalow worth £3,000. In addition, she told another witness, two days before the murder, that she'd got to go home to "lay the old lady out". However, after the handbag was given to Mrs Hands, it found its way to the Merrifields' solicitor, who promptly claimed it was privileged, although later it was handed over. At this point, the spoon had been found. The trial saw 45 prosecution witnesses, while Manchester Assizes heard how a bottle of rum was used to mask the taste and smell of the rat poison that killed the victim. However, the QC defending the accused couple stated on 23rd July 1953 that he would call evidence that proved that Sarah died of natural causes. Mr J Nahum told the court: "Professor Webster will tell you it is his firm opinion that the old lady did not die of phosphorus poisoning – but from necrosis of the liver, due to natural causes." Professor Webster was described as "one of Britain's foremost forensic science experts", but Dr George Manning, a Home Office pathologist, said that, in his opinion, death was due to heart failure caused by phosphorus poisoning. Both husband and wife pleaded not guilty to poisoning their employer, and throughout the trial Alfred Merrifield showed a great deal of emotion in court. In his evidence, he told the court that he had not been a party to the insurance policies that his wife had taken out. In fact, he said he hadn't even known of them until proceedings began.

On 30th July, in his final speech to the jury, Sir Lionel Heald said: "Poisoning has always been a crime of the deepest dye because of its treacherous and secret character." He continued: "I put it quite bluntly, suicide and accident are right out of the picture altogether – it can be nothing but murder." Defending counsel described Mrs Merrifield as "a tragic simpleton, and no more capable of taking part in this foul scheme than a child". On 31st July, Alfred Merrifield was taken from the dock to leave his wife to face the death sentence alone. After being out five hours and 43 minutes, the jury found Louisa Merrifield guilty of poisoning Sarah Ann Ricketts. However, they failed to agree on a verdict with regard to Alfred and he was ordered to be retried, although that was unlikely, according to reports at the time. The Director of Public Prosecutions was more likely to discharge the accused man before he faced a jury for the second time. Mr Merrifield stumbled down the steps, seemingly bewildered and unaware of what was happening as the jury's verdicts were disclosed. As his footsteps echoed down the underground passage, the judge slowly donned his black cap. Mrs Merrifield whispered, when asked, that she had nothing further to say. Then Mr Justice Glyn-Jones said gravely: "You have been convicted on plain evidence of as wicked and cruel a murder as I ever heard tell of." As he sentenced Louisa Merrifield to death he said: "May the Lord have mercy on your soul." She was then taken to the condemned cell, while her husband was sent to the hospital at Strangeways prison in Manchester.

Scores of people jammed the darkened streets outside the court building where they had waited for hours. Inside the building, the judge thanked the QCs for their handling of the case, particularly John Budd, the solicitor who had instructed the defence counsel. The judge also explained that Mrs Merrifield had just 10 days in which to appeal her sentence.

Forty-one years before this trial, in a similar case, Frederick Henry Seddon, who stood accused with his wife, Margaret, of poisoning their lodger, Eliza Barrow, in London, was found guilty. Margaret Seddon was found not guilty. In the Merrifield case, for the first time in history, only the wife was found guilty and condemned to death. As the *Mirror* wrote: "She was never an attractive woman – plump, with untidy hair, thick woollen stockings, dowdy clothes and spectacles. Yet Louisa Merrifield, mother of nine children, had one charm – the power to make old men and women trust her with their money and their lives. And, it changed a drab, ordinary working-class housewife, daughter of a miner, into a ruthless, cold-blooded, calculating poisoner."

At the age of 25 she married iron dresser Joseph Ellison in Wigan, her hometown, and settled down to have four children. After a few years of marriage, she found she wanted something else – money, excitement, and much more than her husband could provide on £4 10s a week. She went into business and opened two shops, but both failed. Then she turned to petty crime, stealing neighbours' ration books and selling them. For that she faced jail, but after her release she discovered that old men liked her company and old women trusted her. She met retired colliery manager, Richard Weston, who lived in a smart semi-detached house. He was 78 and, when his wife died, Louisa made her move. Within weeks of him lodging with Merrifield and her then husband, Joseph Ellison died. The coroner could not pinpoint the cause of death and cited it was natural causes. Louisa mourned for two months before she married Weston. Eight weeks later he was dead. A week after his funeral, she met Alfred Merrifield, a lonely widower. He offered good prospects and followed in Weston's footsteps to the register office. However, Merrifield's money didn't last long and Louisa became disillusioned. The couple were quite quickly evicted for rent arrears. They moved to Blackpool where Louisa Merrifield worked many different jobs – and took out insurances on her husband secretly. In the meantime the couple fought and bickered their way from one dingy boarding house to another while Louisa combed the "Help Wanted" ads for lonely old people.

After the Sarah Ricketts case, on 6th August 1953, Alfred Merrifield was released from jail and returned to the bungalow, where he told reporters: "I have been through the shadow of the gallows." It transpired that Heald had decided to direct an entry of "nolle prosequi" against him, which meant that the Crown was unwilling to prosecute. Meanwhile, Louisa Merrifield had lodged an appeal against the death sentence. Her execution, at that time fixed for 18th August, was postponed, so that her appeal could be heard in London on 1st September. The grounds for the appeal, given that there was no new evidence, was cited to be the "alleged misdirection of the jury". In no previous cases, argued her QC, had there been a complete failure to connect the appellant with obtaining poison, but the judge did not give the jury any direction during the trial with regard to the fact that Louisa could not be linked to the poison. However, the appeal was dismissed by three judges on 3rd September 1953. Rejecting the plea that Justice Glyn-Jones had misdirected the jury, the president of the Court of Criminal Appeal, Mr Justice Cassels, said: "This court is satisfied there was no miscarriage of justice." At the time, no poisoner had ever been given a reprieve for murder as the act of poisoning was regarded as "too vicious for mercy". Hearing the words of the judge proved too much for the condemned woman, who leapt to her feet with her fact contorted. She flung up an arm and muttered through clenched teeth: "I am innocent." Her fate rested with the Home Secretary, Sir David Maxwell-Fyfe. While Britain had a long history of aversion to hanging women, there was an even greater "horror" when it came to poisoners. The Home Secretary was to be asked to advise the Queen to exercise the royal prerogative of mercy after the appeal failed. On 16th September 1953, it was reported that the Home Secretary had refused the reprieve. After being told the news, Louisa Merrifield asked to speak with her husband, whom she had refused to see on three prior occasions.

On 17th September, Alfred Merrifield said farewell to his wife. In a bare room at Strangeways, he faced her across a wooden table with a partition down the middle. When they reached out their hands to touch for the last time, warders brushed them apart. The following day, at 9.00am, Louisa Merrifield was executed at the gallows. On 1st October, it was reported that in the "death cell", the day before she was hanged, Merrifield drew up a will disinheriting her husband. She left all her personal possessions to her son, Oswald Ellison. Three years later it was announced that Alfred Merrifield was to share in the will of the widow that his wife was executed for killing. He was to get one-sixth of the £2,000 estate left by Sarah Ricketts.

Styllou Christofi

1954

It was nearly midnight, a court was told, when John Young looked into a neighbour's garden where a fire was burning. He watched as a woman bent over what appeared to be a wax model in the fire. And, by the light from a kitchen window, he thought he recognized the woman he could see as Styllou Christofi. Young believed her to be burning rubbish. What he did not know was that he was watching what the prosecution said was the last act of a murder "drama". The "wax model" was actually the murderer's daughter-in-law, German-born Hella Christofi, 36, claimed the prosecution at Hampstead, London, where Styllou Christofi was accused of murder in August 1954.

Mr J P Claxton, prosecuting, gave a "dramatic" reconstruction of how the police believed that Hella died at her home in South Hill Park Road, Hampstead, on the night of 29th July that same year. She had been hit over the head first and then strangled. A bloodstained ash-plate from a boiler in the house was suspected of being used to cause the head injuries, while a scarf belonging to one of the victim's three children had been used to strangle her. An attempt had been made to burn the body in the yard behind the house. Claxton said: "Around the body was a lot of charred paper and wood that had been well soaked in paraffin. It was around 11.45pm that Mr Young saw Mrs Christofi in her garden near the fire." The time was important because the accused said she'd found her dead daughter-in-law at around 1.00am. "Her explanation," said Claxton, "is that she woke about 1.00am, that she smelt burning, that she went downstairs, saw the body in the area, went out and sought help. That is the explanation she has given and which she has stuck to all along." John Young, who lived two doors away, told the court that he first noticed that the whole of the back of the Christofi house was aglow, "as though from the light of a fire. I called out, but got no reply," he said, "and I called my wife into the garden, I crossed the intervening garden and looked into the area. I saw a fire and what I took to be a wax model lying on it. It was surrounded by flames. The arms were raised and bent back at the elbow, like some of the models you see in shop windows. I looked into the kitchen through the French windows. I saw a figure there move around the table and come out into the area. She bent over the body, and gave me the impression she was about to stir the fire up." He added: "I thought it was in order and returned to my house." Hella's husband, wine waiter Stavros Christofi, a Cypriot, told the court that he was at work when his wife died. As he gave evidence, he didn't once look towards his mother, who sat in the dock with a black silk scarf draped over her dark hair. Stavros said that his mother had lived with them for about a year. She was unable to speak English and she did not get on well with his wife he told the court. About three weeks before his wife's death, he and Hella had talked with his mother, and it was arranged that she should return to Cyprus. When asked, Stavros confirmed that his mother wasn't exactly happy with the decision, but said: "If you feel that way, I'll go back." The bereaved husband began to sob as he was asked to identify his wife's gold wedding ring, which was alleged to have been hidden behind an ornament in his mother's bedroom. Then he said: "Yes, it is my wife's ring. It has always been a tight fit. The ring could never have fallen off her finger. She had never removed it herself before." The couple had been married for 13 years, yet Styllou told police that she found the ring on the stairs and thought it was a curtain ring. Claxton added: "You will hear from the police that there is not a curtain ring in that house." Harry Burstoff, from Cricklewood, told the court that Styllou Christofi ran up to his car at about 1.00am on 29th July and said: "Please come. Fire burning. Children sleeping." He and his wife returned to the house with her and he said: "Where is the fire." He continued by saying that Christofi had told him to "Ssh!" as the "babies" were sleeping. At the same time, she opened another door and just stood, while Mrs Burstoff suddenly gave a shout and said: "Look, there is somebody on the floor."

"I looked and saw only a head covered with blood." He then called the police before going outside with his wife and Christofi, whom he alleged then stated: "Me smell burning. Me come down. Me pour water, but she be died." When asked who the body was, the accused said: "My son marry Germany girl he like. Plenty clothes, plenty shoes. Babies going to Germany." At the trial, 53-year-old Styllou Christofi was described by her counsel as "absolutely bewildered by these proceedings". Defending counsel

Mr Vardy asked an interpreter to tell the accused that he was there "to watch her interests".

On 25th October 1954, the jury at the murder trial at the Old Bailey was told by Christmas Humphreys, prosecuting, that it was "a stupid murder by a stupid woman of the illiterate peasant type". He added: "She really believed that after washing the floor she could eliminate bloodstains, and that with a small tin of paraffin, she could burn a body so that it could not be recognised." Christofi pleaded not guilty to the murder of Hella. However, Humphreys said that Hella died from strangulation, caused by a scarf. The scarf was cut into four pieces. Three were found under some wet ashes in the dustbin, but a fourth was found in the yard. "So this is a murderess who is remarkably tidy in clearing away the evidence of the murder," he stated. The 10 men and two women on the jury were taken to the "house of death" on 26th October. It was dark and it was raining. The jurors stood near a waist-high wall and looked down into the concrete area where the charred body of Hella Christofi had been found. For 40 minutes they tried to picture the scene that John Young had described, as directed by Mr Justice Devlin. John Young had looked over the wall, into the garden of number 11, where he saw the accused. After looking into the "area" as Mr Young had done, at night, the jurors were taken upstairs to a bedroom, where the accused said she was sleeping at the time of the fire. On 27th October, Styllou Christofi took to the witness box where a hushed court heard her deny that she was jealous of her late daughter-in-law. Three times she was heard to say: "Oudepote", meaning "never" in response to the prosecutor's questions.

On 28th October 1954, Styllou Christofi waited for the second time for a jury to decide whether she should live or die. Twenty-nine years previously, at the age of 24, she had stood in the dock in Famagusta, Cyprus, with two other women. All three had been charged with the murder of Christofi's mother-in-law who had died after a burning stake of wood had been forced into her mouth. All three were found not guilty. However, at the court at the Old Bailey, Christofi was found guilty of murdering her daughter-in-law, Hella. It took the jury two hours to reach their damning verdict. The convicted killer was then sentenced to death before being taken to the condemned cell. An interpreter had stood in the well of the court beneath the dock to translate the verdict for her.

Christofi's appeal was launched on 1st November 1954, but when it was heard at the end of the month, it failed in just four minutes. The Court of Criminal Appeal dismissed the appeal against the conviction after the murderer's counsel, Mr D Weitzman, QC, said that, having studied the case, he had been unable to find any point of appeal to make to the court. Christofi was to be executed on 15th December at Holloway, but MPs made an "11th-hour" bid to save the condemned woman the night before the hanging. Led by Sir Leslie Plummer and Sydney Silverman, MPs tried to get the Home Secretary, Lloyd George, to accept dramatic evidence from Dr Thomas Christie, the principle doctor at Holloway jail, that Christofi was suffering from a brain disease. They believed that if the doctor's evidence had been put before the jury, it might have meant the woman was found guilty but insane.

The execution, however, went ahead as planned, and for the first time in British criminal history, a female governor oversaw the hanging. Dr Charity Taylor, 39, Governor of Holloway, was present when Styllou Christofi went to the scaffold.

Ruth Ellis

1955

"She was a leading mannequin. He was a crack car racing driver" wrote the *Mirror*. Ruth Ellis, 28, and David Blakely, 25, were the "picture of happiness", but on 20th April 1955 Ellis stood in the dock of a London court accused of Blakely's murder. David was found shot dead outside a Hampstead pub on Easter Sunday. Ellis, a former West End club manager, and the divorced wife of a dental surgeon, was in the dock for just two minutes. Chief Inspector Leslie Davies asked for a remand and said the prosecution would be ready to proceed with the case the following week. Mr J Rickford, defending, then asked for a copy of a statement alleged to have been made by Ellis to the police. He also asked for a list of prosecution witnesses. At a special sitting of the magistrates on Easter Monday when Ellis was first charged, Davies said that she made a statement. David Blakely, son of a Sheffield doctor, was educated at Shrewsbury Public School and served as a lieutenant in the Highland Light Infantry. He was due to drive an Emperor HRG racing car at Goodwood on Easter Monday, but he never made it to the track.

Ellis was found standing over the body of motorist David with a revolver in her hand. It was the end of a romance that had begun two years earlier in the Little Club, in Knightsbridge, London. Described as a model, Ellis was accused of murder. The couple began living together shortly after they met. Ellis had lost her first husband, with whom she had a child, during the war. She had a further child with her second husband, whom she divorced in 1954. Mr J Claxton, prosecuting, told the court on 28th April 1955 that Ellis was friendly with a man called Desmond Cussen, and went to live with him after a falling out with Blakely, just before Christmas 1954. "She had in fact, told Mr Cussen that she had finished with Blakely, and she and Mr Cussen continued to live together [at a flat in Devonshire Street, Marylebone], although it would appear that from time to time she still went out with Blakely," said the prosecutor. But all was not well, and as a result of a phone call from Blakely in January 1955 to Anthony Findlater, a friend with whom he was building a car, Findlater went to Cussen's flat. He took another friend, Mr Gunnell, with him. There they found Blakely and Ellis, and David told his friends that he wished to leave his former lover and break off all association with her. However, he also told them that she wouldn't let him. Ellis was at this time in a highly emotional, almost hysterical condition. In February, it seemed that Blakely and Ellis decided to live together again, because on the ninth of the month she rented a furnished apartment in Egerton Gardens, in Kensington. There they lived together as man and wife, according to Claxton, and Blakely was known to the landlady as Mr Ellis. Once he left each morning, Mr Cussen would visit the flat and he and Ellis would go out. At the beginning of April, Blakely and Ellis attended a race meeting in Chester with Findlater and his wife, and, on Good Friday, Blakely went to his friend's flat in Tanza Road, Hampstead, and, at his suggestion, was going to spend the weekend there. "In the course of that day, and in the early hours of the following day, Mrs Ellis was fairly constantly on the telephone. She kept on ringing up wanting to know if Blakely was there," said Claxton. "Having regard to what Findlater knew of a previous experience, when he had to go to Cussen's flat and rescue Blakely from Mrs Ellis, he told her that Blakely was not there," he continued. Early the next morning Ellis was banging on the front door of the flat and ringing the bell to such an extent that the police were called. By the time the police arrived, Ellis had gone.

What happened next came on the day of the alleged shooting. The Findlaters, Gunnell and Blakely were having a party in the Tanza Road flat before the former lover and Gunnell went off to the Magdala pub for more beer. In the pub was an off-duty police officer, who saw a woman who he identified as Ruth Ellis looking in through the window. The two men left with the beer, then Gunnell heard two shots and saw Blakely lying face down on the pavement. Gunnell then saw Ellis fire more shots into Blakely's back said the prosecutor. Only two bullet wounds were found in the murdered victim's body, but there were six empty cartridge cases in the gun. Later, said Mr Claxton, Mrs Ellis told officers at Hampstead police station: "I am guilty. I am rather confused. It all started about two years ago when I met David Blakely at the Little Club ..." However, when Ellis was sent for trial she pleaded not guilty. She reserved her defence. On 20th June 1955, Ruth Ellis sobbed at the Old

Bailey when she was shown a large photograph. Written on the photo was: "To Ruth, with all my love, David." She was asked by Christmas Humphreys, prosecuting: "When you fired that revolver into the body of David Blakely what did you intend to do?" She replied: "It was obvious I meant to kill him." But she still pleaded not guilty. Her defence counsel, Mr Melford Stevenson, QC, told the jury: "It is open to you to say the offence of which she is guilty is not murder but manslaughter." Ellis, he said, had been "the subject of emotional disturbance and [was] temporarily unseated in her judgment". He asked her to tell the court the "long, painful and sometimes sordid story" of her life with Blakely up to the time of his death. Although Ellis was married at the time she met Blakely, the two became lovers within two weeks of meeting. The court was told how later she made "numerous efforts" to end the affair and get Blakely out of her flat. In December 1954, she moved in with Desmond Cussen. However, the previous affair never really ended. Blakely arrived at the flat on Christmas night and there was a scene. Asked why she still saw Blakely, Ellis said she was still in love with him. She confirmed that she'd made no further efforts to effectively end the relationship. Ellis also admitted that she'd had to confront Blakely over his relationships with other women. She claimed that she had ended up with a sprained ankle, bruises and a black eye after an altercation with her lover, and when asked what led to the row said that they had been drinking quite a lot and they had returned to Cussen's flat where there had been a "scene". David Blakely then sent her some flowers with a card which read: "Sorry, darling. I love you, David." It was after that that Ellis secured the rented apartment for them in Kensington, moving in on 9th February. There was then some "trouble" with another woman living in Penn, Buckinghamshire. Ellis told the court that Cussen had driven her down to Penn on one occasion, where she had found her lover with the woman. She had remained outside the house all night and watched as Blakely left at 9.00am the following morning. He had parked his car out of sight, around the corner behind a public house. Ellis was asked how she felt at the time. "I was jealous of him now. Before he had been jealous of me, but it was my turn now to be jealous of him," she admitted. Mr Stevenson asked: "In March did you find you were pregnant?" "Yes," came the reply. Ellis then described how Blakely had become extremely violent towards her. She admitted to shooting her lover dead, but denied murder.

Neither the defence counsel nor the accused questioned the fact that Ellis had shot her lover. That was evident, but the reasons as to why and the duress she was under at the time were called into question. Stevenson said: "The law of England, in its mercy, provides that if a person has been the subject of such emotional disturbance she is for the time being unseated in her judgment, it is open for you ... to [find] she is guilty ... [of] manslaughter. That is what we, on her behalf, ask you to do in this case." He added: "Her story is a long one story, a painful story, and – as you will find in some ways – a sordid story. You have nothing to do with morals. The question you have to decide yes or no is whether or not this woman is guilty of brutal murder." The defence barrister said: "You will hear the sad story of her association with this young man who is now dead. He was a most unpleasant person. The fact stands out like a beacon that this young man became an absolute necessity to this young woman. She found herself in something like an emotional prison guarded by this young man, from which there seemed to be no escape." Ellis then gave her evidence after the prosecution witnesses described how they saw her empty six rounds of the revolver at Blakely. She said that her marriage had been dissolved and that she was the mother of two children, a boy of 10 and a girl of three. At first, when arriving to live with Ellis, Blakely had seemed quite devoted. However, after a short time, Blakely became prone to regular violent outbursts. Ellis tried to break off the relationship, but her lover ignored her requests. The dead man was reported as being a heavy drinker; drinking often preceded the onset of violence. Ellis told the court: "When I put the gun in my bag, I intended to find David and shoot him. I took a taxi to Tanza Road. As I arrived, David's car drove away from the Findlaters' address. I dismissed the taxi and walked down the road to the nearest pub, where I noticed David's car outside. I waited till he came out with a friend I knew as Clive, that is, Gunnell. David went to his car door and opened it. I was a little way away from it. He turned and saw me and then turned away from me. I took the gun from my bag and shot him. He turned and ran a few steps round the car. I thought I had missed him so I fired again. He was still running and I fired a third shot. I do not remember firing any more, but I must have done. I remember he was lying on the footpath and I was standing beside him. He was bleeding badly and it seemed ages before the ambulance came. A man came up and I said: 'Will you call the ambulance and the police?' He said: 'I am a policeman.'" Following this, Mr Humphreys said: "Whatever the background and whatever may have been in her mind at the time she took that gun, if you have no doubt she took the gun with the object of finding and shooting David Blakely, in my submission your only verdict can be wilful murder." The case continued.

Ruth Ellis was allowed to see her father before she was taken to a condemned cell on 21st June 1955. He had buried his head in his hands at the Old Bailey and wept quietly as the 28-year-old girl he had brought up in a Manchester backstreet was sentenced to death for the shooting of her 25-year-old lover, David Blakely. He made his way sadly down to the cells beneath No. 1 Court. For an hour he talked there with Ruth Ellis, the daughter who had left him in her teens for the bright lights of London's West End. A few moments beforehand, Ellis had listened impassively as Mr Justice Havers said: "The jury have convicted you of murder. In my view it is the only possible verdict." In fact, Ruth Ellis remained the calmest person in the crowded court. She smiled as she heard the foreman of the jury announce the verdict of "guilty". And she smiled again after she was given the death sentence. She was then led to the cells. It had been dramatic, but it was one of the quickest murder trials ever recorded. It was all over in one and a half days and neither the Crown nor the defence made a final

Women Killers

speech. The jury took just 23 minutes to convict Ruth Ellis, and there was no recommendation for mercy.

The jury of 10 men and two women was not in court after giving its verdict, when the judge told the court that there should be no "sympathy" for a woman who had murdered out of "jealousy". The judge had ordered that the jury should approach the case with neither sympathy for the dead man nor for the woman in court accused of his murder. Dealing with the legal definition of murder, the judge continued: "In our law, murder is the unlawful killing of one person by another with malice. Malice means the formation of the intention either to kill or to do grievous bodily harm. Long premeditation is unnecessary. But there must be the intent to kill or to do grievous bodily harm. In considering such matters the jury should have regard to the type of weapon that was used, and number of shots fired and all the circumstances of the case. In this case, six shots were fired by a Smith and Wesson revolver, a lethal weapon." He continued: "If you are satisfied Ellis intentionally fired the shot or shots, then that would amount to a verdict of guilty of murder." The defence put forward by Stevenson that Ellis suffered extreme provocation during her relationship with Blakely was dismissed by the judge. He placed his black cap on his head as he sentenced the woman to die.

Ellis was barely out of her teens when she left Manchester for the excitement of London. It took just 12 years to turn into "bitter disillusionment for the girl from the backstreets who hankered after the bright lights". As an attractive woman with a good figure Ellis became a model, posing for scantily clad postcard photographs. The closest she came to her dream of owning a nightclub was an £8-a-week job as manager of the Little Club, a plush afternoon drinking den. It transpired that the American father of her son was never actually her husband, although she always described him as such. He was tragically killed during the Second World War. She then married Norman Ellis and had a daughter, but Norman divorced her on the grounds of "mental cruelty". Norman was granted custody of the couple's child, and Ruth Ellis drifted back into a life of drinking clubs. Up-and-coming racing driver David Blakely had seemed like her chance at making something of her life. He was rich, handsome and well educated. He was also beginning to make a name for himself and gaining a high profile. His hard drinking was matched only by that of Ellis. She knew that his family would never approve of the match, and he knew he faced disgrace if he married his lover. Ellis, it was claimed, tried every trick in the book to try and marry Blakely. She began French lessons and took a speech course to lose her northern accent, but all she gained in her fight to keep her man was a date with the scaffold. She decided not to appeal her conviction, when only a reprieve from the Home Secretary could save her. The apparent unconcern of the girl who could smile when sentenced to death, and later calmly reject an appeal that might commute her sentence to life, surprised even the most hardened of women officials at Holloway prison, where Ellis was held in the condemned cell. Ellis gave instructions that her expensive wardrobe of evening gowns and clothes should be sold and the proceeds used to provide for her son. However, despite the fact Ellis did not want to appeal, Lloyd George, the Home Secretary, was to review all the papers and then make a decision about Ellis and her future. He would decide whether she lived or died.

It was announced by the Home Office on 24th June 1955 that Ellis' execution date had been set for 13th July. Her legal advisors were expected to make a special plea, which the Home Secretary would study before the execution date. Reporters wrote constantly in the press about whether Ellis should be allowed to die. "Should Ruth Ellis Hang?" they asked. The prospect of the gallows did not stop the use of the gun, the knife and the fatal blow they argued. It didn't even stop the strangler's hands or the poisoner, more likely to meet their fate at the scaffold. One reporter, despite the terrible crime as he called it, was vehemently opposed to Ruth Ellis being executed. He said: "This was a murder of love and hate. The one as fierce as the other – the storm of tenderness matching the fury of revenge. In human nature, where passion is involved, love and hate walk hand in hand and side by side." He continued: "There was no slow poisoning, but a sudden explosion of forces of evil that are latent in the hearts of more men and women than would care to admit it – terrible, senseless evil, and all too human." He spoke of public opinion and wrote: "By the nature of her crime, by the nature of her appearance, by the ingrained horror that most people have at the prospect of a woman shortly to be dragged to the scaffold, it is inevitable that millions of people will be increasingly drawn towards the shortening shadow of the hideous event to come. Some will be fascinated – morbidly so. Others will be horrified and haunted. But there will be an almost tribal unanimity in the interest of the case. It is part of the degrading price that capital punishment demands – and always gets. Justice not only has to be done, but it also has to be seen to be done. And so have the barbaric penalties of execution. They too have to be seen to be done. This ghastly business, this obscene ritual which we, who claim to be the most civilised people in the world, have never succeeded in getting rid of, is witnessed by many people – most of whom have the decency to want to vomit."

Petitions closed four days before the planned execution and were sent to the Home Office. However, Ellis was refused a reprieve on 11th July. She would face the gallows. The reporter defiantly against the hanging, known only as Cassandra (real name William Connor), was appalled that on a beautiful day in July 1955, at 9.00am in the morning, Ruth Ellis would meet her death. He wrote: "A bag of sand will have been filled to the same weight as the condemned woman and it will have been left hanging overnight to stretch the rope." There had been a dramatic last-minute appeal to save Ellis by Victor Mishcon, a Labour MP and leading solicitor, and it was believed that Ellis told him details behind the murder that had not been heard before. It was cited that "someone" could have come forward to save her, and didn't. Ruth Ellis was visited the day before her execution by her parents and a friend, Jacqueline Dyer. Following the execution, a debate raged across the media about whether the time had come to abolish hanging in Britain. Meanwhile, the media also reported that Ruth Ellis was the "calmest woman who ever went to the gallows". She refused breakfast, but accepted a glass of brandy from a warder. As she sipped it she asked calmly if she would be blindfolded. She was told gently that a white hood would be placed over her head. The execution entourage arrived at her cell and she was duly escorted at one minute to nine. The mother of two calmly walked with the entourage to the execution chamber. Seconds later, she was dead.

Many countries around the world stated that Ruth Ellis should never have hanged. Australian media said it shamed Britain, while in the USA there were commentaries splashed across the front pages saying it should never have been allowed. In Sweden, the British were openly slammed and judged. One newspaper said: "The continuance of the death sentence in England is a burden for England's good name in the world."

Britain sat up, took responsibility and finally took notice. On 16th February 1956, after six and a half hours of debate, MPs voted by 293 votes to 262 – a majority of 31 – that hanging should be abolished. Ruth Ellis was the last woman to make the terrifying, if short, walk to the gallows in Britain, and due to her crime of passion her name was sealed in legislative history for all time.

How times change. In the 21st century Ruth Ellis would have been considered a battered woman, a woman so "groomed" and "controlled" that the case would probably have been considered on a lesser charge. Just 10 days before she shot Blakely, the abusive man had punched Ruth in the stomach, causing her to miscarry. In 2003, the London Appeal Court was given the facts of the case and was told that Ellis suffered from "battered woman syndrome" as it was called. A modern-day jury would probably have been directed to consider a verdict of manslaughter. Blakely, it was revealed, had beaten Ruth "unmercifully". However, even in 2003 the Crown argued that Ruth Ellis "deserved to die" for the murder, because, as the law stood at the time the crime was committed, the death penalty was still in place. In 2005, it was revealed that the convicted murderer had secretly been denied a pardon by the Government. One of the real tragedies of the story has to be the story of Ruth's devastated son, Clare McCallum, who was just 10 years old at the time of his mother's death. He never got over what happened, and despite the best efforts of family members around him he turned to a life of drugs and suffered from depression. He was found dead in his Paddington flat at the age of 37, surrounded by tablets and empty bottles. He had died as a result of a drug overdose. He was buried next to his mother's grave in Old Amersham, Buckinghamshire. It was a terrible end to a tragic case, with the deaths of two people, and an unborn baby, brought about by the actions of one abusive man.

Yvonne Jennion

1958

On 10th October 1958, Yvonne Jennion was accused of murdering her aunt. The 23-year-old from St Helens, Lancashire, had allegedly hit 53-year-old Ivy Vye over the head with a brass ashtray before strangling the woman to death. Jennion, an unemployed cook, showed no emotion as she sat in the dock and heard Chief Superintendent James Ball tell how the incident was alleged to have happened. Ball said that Yvonne went to her aunt's home in St Helens and that after "they had been sitting, talking for a time, some altercation took place between them". He said that Vye's body, with head injuries and a cord round the neck, was found by her husband George when he arrived home for lunch. Jennion was asked if she objected to being remanded in custody. "No," came the reply. Jennion was jailed for life in Manchester in 1958, but in April 1966 she and two other women escaped from Askham Grange open prison in Yorkshire.

Norma Everson

1961

When Winifred Lord, 44, a mother of two, was found stabbed to death in Highbury, London, in 1961, the woman found guilty of her untimely death was named as 33-year-old van driver Norma Everson. She appeared before magistrates on 19th June. Another woman who shared a flat with Everson was also interviewed. She had to be treated for a minor head injury, but was able to help police. Everson was convicted, but five years later, in June 1966, just two months after Jennion escaped from prison, this woman too was on the run. Like Jennion, she escaped with two other convicted criminals – a "gun girl" and "a trickster". The women dodged through a hole in a fence and fled as they were being led out for the Sunday evening leisure hour at the prison in Styal, Cheshire. Freedom lasted just seven hours. Just before midnight, the women were seen near a local farm by John and Christopher Dennis, two brothers who were taking their dog for a walk. While Christopher kept an eye on the women, John telephoned police and detectives with dogs surrounded the field where the women were seen. Everson served life for murder.

Myra Hindley
(with Ian Brady)

1963

Police moved round a fairground on 28th December 1964 asking: "Have you seen this little girl?" They took with them a picture of 10-year-old Lesley Downey, who had vanished after a visit to the fair on Boxing Day. The photograph, taken earlier that month, showed Lesley, from Ancoats, Manchester, with Father Christmas. What started as a routine search for a missing child was going to lead police to one of the biggest manhunts Britain had ever seen, the deaths of innocent children and the conviction of two of the country's worst ever serial murderers, Myra Hindley and Ian Brady.

Lesley went to the fair with Linda Clarke, aged eight, and her little sister, aged just four. Linda said: "We spent out money on a Cyclone Ride, then set off home, but Lesley changed her mind and went back alone to the fair." Police were at this point seriously worried about her safety. Superintendent Philip Machent said: "We have not given up hope of finding her alive, but it is beginning to look grim."

Almost a year later, shorthand typist Myra Hindley, 23, appeared in court on 11th October 1965, on a charge of harbouring a man accused of murder. The murder victim was 17-year-old Edward Evans. He was said to have been found dead the week before at a house in Wardle Brook Avenue in Greater Manchester.

Police Superintendent Robert Talbot said that a man had been charged with murder. The charge against Hindley, of Wardle Brook Avenue, Hattersley, said that she "Well knowing that Ian Brady had murdered Edward Evans, did receive, comfort, harbour, assist and maintain the said Ian Brady." She was remanded in custody for a week and allowed legal aid as it was then called. On 12th October, top detectives reopened the files on eight missing people, including three children, after receiving information that pointed to a multiple murderer. The information led teams of detectives to the wild moors on the Cheshire–Yorkshire border. They were waiting for the vital "pinpoint clue" which would tell them where to dig for a body – and possibly more than one. Among the missing people were three children whose disappearances had sparked huge police searches.

John Kilbride was 12 when he disappeared from his home in Ashton-under-Lyne, Lancashire, on Saturday 23rd November 1963. He was last seen in the local marketplace. The other children were Keith Bennett, 12, of Eston Street, Chorlton-on-Medlock, Manchester, who had disappeared on 16th June 1964, and Lesley Downey. Chief Superintendent Douglas Nimmo, head of Manchester CID, Detective Chief Superintendent Harold Prescott, head of Lancashire CID, and Detective Chief Superintendent Arthur Benfield, head of Cheshire CID, held an urgent meeting on the new development. Meanwhile, on the bracken-covered moors and hills of the Peak District National Park, detectives with cameras searched alongside the main Manchester–Sheffield road, half a mile from Woodhead. Detectives were told a body was buried here. They were also interested in another area at Penistone, 11 miles away. The mothers of all three missing children waited anxiously for news. Mrs Sheila Kilbride summed up what they were all feeling: "I want to know if it is my little boy who is on the moor. It is dreadful to keep on living with this ... not knowing whether he is alive or dead. The police have not been to see me. I will wait." Keith Bennett had been on the way to see his grandmother when he went missing. His mother, Mrs Winifred Bennett, said: "The strain has been awful. To know one way or the other – whether the boy is alive or dead – would be a relief." She added: "I am convinced, and so is his grandmother, that he is still alive, but we don't know where. This week, detectives came to the house and showed us a photograph of a man. They assured us they are still looking for Keith." The young boy was last seen in Stockport Road, Longsight, not far from his home. Mrs Bennett said: "We hope that these inquiries are going to show us where Keith is." Meanwhile, Ann Downey still clung to the hope that her daughter was alive: "I believe that somewhere my little girl is safe and well. The police haven't been to see me. But, every now and again, I go into Manchester and call at the police station where the search was centred."

As the investigations continued, police probed every corner of a "house of secrets" in the hunt that they considered could uncover the activities of a serial killer, and, by 14th October, 35 miles away, police began digging on moorland. The dramatic steps were taken in an all-out effort to solve the mystery of the eight missing people, who had all disappeared in the Manchester area during the previous three years. Police scientists accompanied detectives to a small, smoke-blackened terraced house where they stayed for several hours – tearing up old floorboards, probing behind chimneys, searching the rafters and prodding the ground under the house. Tests were made on wall surfaces and dust was collected from crevices. The dust samples and pieces of floorboard were to be examined in the police laboratory in Preston. It was hoped that scientists could prove whether any of the eight people had ever been in the house. Police across the region were asked to examine all files dealing with suspicious cars on the moors during the previous three years too, and one type of vehicle had been mentioned in particular.

Detectives spent six hours carrying out a survey and digging on the moors, but brought the day's activities to an end as dusk fell. As 150 men packed up, Detective Chief Inspector Joe Mounsey said they wouldn't be searching the moor again unless there was fresh evidence. However, a huge new search for buried bodies began in earnest on 18th October 1965 after Lesley Downey's body was found in a lonely, shallow grave. On a cold Saturday night, just days before, by the yellow light of sodium lamps, a police squad found the grave in a mound of peaty mould and earth, 1,400 feet up in the Pennine hills, 200 yards from the A635 at Wessenden Head, in Yorkshire's West Riding. Near the body, the missing child's clothes were found – a tartan frock, a pink cardigan, brown buckled shoes and striped stockings. In a little mortuary at Uppermill, two miles from Lesley's "grave", the body was examined by a Home Office pathologist, Professor Cyril Polson. Lesley's mother was driven to the mortuary from her home, and she spent 12 minutes there. The following day, the newspapers reported on another disappearance.

Pauline Reade disappeared quietly, without much fuss. Nobody except her family and the police took very much notice. It was thought she had walked out on her family and started a new life in another town. But after Lesley's body was found, the file on Pauline was reopened. The 16-year-old had simply vanished one night on her way to a dance. On that fateful night, she told her mother she was going to a dance only half a mile away from home in Gorton, Manchester. Carrying 10 shillings, given to her by her parents to buy lemonade and crisps, she gave them no concerns that she wouldn't be coming back. The date was 12th July 1963. Although detectives made a thorough investigation they failed to find "the girl in the pink dress". Like the other mothers, Joan Reade, the missing girl's mother, had not given up hope of finding her daughter alive.

At around the same time, police obtained photographs which they believed could lead them to more moorland graves. The search area – 100 square miles – saw detectives trying to pinpoint the graves they believed they would find from the photographs. They planned to show the enlarged photos to shepherds and hill farmers. Detectives also once again swooped on a quiet terraced house. It was the second house of secrets to be examined by the police. Afterwards, Joe Mounsey took away boxes containing articles to the murder investigation headquarters. The case was, by now, dubbed the "bodies on the moor", and a team of CID men from five police forces was piecing together the details of how the victims were lured to their deaths. How they were given a false sense of security. How young boys and girls became drunk on wine. How they were then killed. And how their bodies were disposed of. It was then disclosed that detectives were trying to discover if torture had been used on any of the victims. Police continued their search of the second house, while 80 policemen searched the moors. In other news, it was reported that a mystery woman had been taken to the moors. She did not leave the car but had pointed out a spot near the road, more than a mile from where Lesley's body was found. The area was then staked off and 12 policemen began digging. Fresh inquiries also began into another missing girl, 16-year-old Pauline Brown who had disappeared from her home in Ardwick, Manchester, in 1960. Police also believed that one 12-year-old girl was lured in and plied with drink by the killer they were seeking, but that she wasn't killed. A tape recording of a little girl talking to a man they believed to be the killer had been discovered by detectives. On 21st October it was reported that charges were likely to be made in connection with the death of Lesley.

Assistant Chief Constable Eric Cunningham, head of the regional crime squad in the northwest, had had talks the previous evening with his two detective chief superintendents. The discussion followed a visit by two senior detectives to a Home Office laboratory that same day, from where they returned with reports to Hyde HQ, in Cheshire. That day, a man and a woman were accused of murdering Lesley Downey. They appeared in court separately. It was the second murder charge against the man known as Ian Brady, 27, a stock clerk of no fixed address. Myra Hindley was also charged with murder, and with harbouring Brady. The court hearing in Hyde lasted eight minutes.

Brady had already been accused of killing Edward Evans, 17, after he was found dead in Wardle Brook Avenue, Hattersley in Hyde, where the murderer was alleged to have lived. The second charge alleged that Brady murdered Lesley between December 1964 and October 1965. When charged with murder, Brady had replied: "Not guilty." After he was led away, Hindley appeared on remand and was charged with murdering Lesley. When accused by police of the murder, she said: "It is not true."

The body of 12-year-old John Kilbride was found in October 1965 in a moorland grave. He was found buried on Saddleworth Moor, near Greenfield, Yorkshire. He had been missing for nearly two years. Lesley had been missing for 10 months when her body was found. John's parents, Patrick and Sheila Kilbride, were driven to the mortuary at Uppermill, but they were not shown their son's remains. They identified a fragment of clothing and a shoe which had been found buried along with the body. On 25th October 1965, forensic scientists investigating John's death examined bloodstains in a house in a Manchester suburb. They had been found splashed on a wall during the seven-hour investigation. The following day, two RAF jets swept over the miles of moors taking 4,000 pictures to help police search for buried bodies. On 6th December 1965, a 15-minute hearing in the prosecution's case against Brady and Hindley took place. A private hearing, requested by Brady's counsel, David Lloyd Jones due to huge public interest, speculation and numerous rumours that made the case such a high-profile one, was refused, as was that by Philip Curtis, acting for Hindley.

In the following days, it was reported that "a plan for the disposal of a dead youth … a proposal for a bank hold-up … shooting practice on the moors … the study of torture and sexual perversions" were all alleged to be part of the pattern in the murder case. Three victims were named – Edward, Lesley and John. Edward, an apprentice engineer, was said to have 14 hatchet wounds on his body. By this time, Brady had been charged with all three murders and Hindley of murdering Edward and Lesley, of knowing Brady had killed John and of harbouring Brady. Their address was given jointly as Wardle Brook Avenue in Hyde. In the second week of December 1965, the court heard how a little girl went onto the moors with Brady – which it was claimed he knew very well indeed – where she was given wine to drink. A tape recording was found in a left luggage office, it was said. It was this little girl that helped police find a spot on the Cheshire moors where Lesley's body was buried. Patricia Hodges, 12, lived next door but one to the accused couple and had been to the moors several times with Hindley and Brady. It also transpired that the prosecution would be playing the court another tape recording – the voice of Lesley –

which had also been found in left luggage. It was Hindley's prayer book that had led police to the recordings and photographs that had convinced them they had their murderers. Hidden in the spine of the book was a left luggage ticket for a Manchester railway station. In it were two suitcases containing books on torture and perversion, two tape recordings, and negatives and photographs. The photographs showed a young girl in various nude poses. "She had a scarf tied tightly around her mouth and the back of her head," said the prosecution. She was identified as Lesley, by her mother. One of the first witnesses was David Smith, 17, Hindley's brother-in-law. Brady was alleged to have boasted to Smith about killing three or four people, although the accused said he'd only given a "vague impression" in order to impress the teenager. He also hinted to Smith that he buried bodies on the moors, but again claimed he had only said it to enhance his image with Hindley's brother-in-law.

However, Hindley bowed her head and sobbed as the tape recordings were played in court and said she was "ashamed". Mr Mars-Jones, QC, also revealed the nude pictures of Lesley. It was the second day of open court proceedings to see if the couple should stand trial. The prosecutor told the court that some of the fingerprints found on the nude photographs were Hindley's. It was also stated that Brady admitted the suitcases were his, but could not remember depositing them at Central Station. Brady further admitted taking the nude photographs of Lesley at his home, and to knowing about the tape recordings. The prosecutor then reminded the court that there was only a distance of 370 yards between the graves of John and Lesley. Suffocation as the cause of death could not be ruled out in either case at that time. One of the photos on the moor, which showed Hindley and was taken by Brady, was at the exact spot where John's body was found to be buried. When queried about this, Brady made no comment. However, he had previously stated to police that he knew who had killed the child, and had admitted to taking the photo of Hindley.

Meanwhile, Smith's evidence included the fact that Brady had lent him a book about the life and ideas of the Marquis de Sade. The two men had also discussed a life of crime as the best way to make money – Brady, it was alleged, was dissatisfied with working for a living. They also discussed guns, of which Smith said Brady had two. He had seen both revolvers on a visit with the accused to the moors when the two men fired them. While giving evidence Smith admitted that he had been convicted of a number of offences – the first when he was 11 – including assault, housebreaking and theft. He also told of the night he was invited to Hindley and Brady's home. In the living room he saw Brady rain blows on Edward Evans and then pull a cord round his neck. The two accused had said it was Smith that killed the teenager, but Smith was insistent that it was Brady who had murdered the boy with an axe before strangling him. After battering Edward, Brady lit a cigarette and picked up a bottle of wine. Smith had a mouthful of wine, but felt sick following the attack. Smith had been invited into the house by Hindley to pick up some miniature wine bottles.

In the kitchen, he was given three wine bottles by Brady, who then walked into the living room, leaving the door open. He heard a scream, followed by another one and ran inside the room, where he stopped just inside the door. "The first thing I saw was Myra on my right, and then this lad lay on the couch, half on and half off," he said. "Brady was stood astride him. I saw the lad looking up at Brady. Brady was hitting him with an axe." As Brady rained blows on Edward's face and shoulders, the teenager screamed in agony said Smith. Edward then hit the floor and tried to drag himself away, but Brady kept on hitting. Smith said he didn't do anything. He was scared. Brady then hit Edward on the back of the head, waited until he groaned, then hit him again. "The lad stopped groaning and he was making a gurgling noise. Brady wrapped a cushion or a piece of cloth around the lad's head." The court was hushed as Smith continued. He described how Brady got a piece of cord and put it around the boy's neck. "Brady started pulling it. The gurgling was still going on but going a lot quieter. It stopped, the noise. He looked up at Myra and he said: 'That's it. It's the messiest yet.'" Smith told the ever quiet courtroom that Brady had repeated: "You dirty bastard", over and over as he strangled Edward Evans to death. Smith also described how there was blood all over the walls, floor and door. Brady ordered Hindley to get a mop and some soapy water. According to Smith, she duly did as she was asked.

After a clean-up, Smith told the court that Brady asked Hindley to get some sheets, some polythene and a large blanket. Again, she did as she was asked. Smith described that, when asked by Brady, he grabbed the young lad's ankles and they lifted him onto the sheet. He said: "I thought in my own mind that if I wanted to get out of the house I would just do anything." He continued: "We then tied Evans up. His arms were crossed on his chest. Brady did that." When trying to move the body, Brady was alleged to have laughed as he said the young lad was a "dead weight". Smith told the court he saw nothing to laugh at, he felt sick. After tidying up, Smith said Hindley made some tea. During the subsequent conversation, Hindley mentioned a time the couple had been on the moor with a body in the back of the minivan. As Brady was off digging a grave, Hindley had been approached by a policeman who had asked her what was the matter as she waited by the side of the road. She had told him that she had wet "sparking plugs", all the while praying that Brady didn't walk up over the hill. Smith then indicated that Brady smiled as he remembered the incident. They didn't move the body of Edward that night because Brady had hurt his ankle. It seemed to annoy him, Smith told the court. The idea was that, the following day, a family pram would be used to move the body and it would then be taken to the moors. Brady did not say where. After the plan was made, Smith was able to leave the house. He ran all the way home. At 6.00am, after talking to his wife, Smith phoned the police.

In an alleged statement by Brady, he admitted to hitting Edward Evans with the hatchet. It was dictated by the accused after the trussed-up body of the teenager was found in a locked room at the

Florence Maybrick

Florence Maybrick was condemned to death for the murder of her husband in 1889 but her sentence was commuted to penal servitude for life, which generally meant a term of 20 years for a well-behaved convict.

The world was mesmerized by the case of Florence Maybrick in the early 20th century. Following her release from prison in 1904, Maybrick stayed with the Sisters of the Epiphany in Truro, Cornwall, before returning to her native America.

Edith Thompson
Percy Thompson and his wife Edith. In October 1922, Percy was found dead on a pavement in Ilford, Essex, and his wife was charged with his murder.

The *Daily Mirror* front page on 6th October 1922 reported on possible witnesses, while police searched the locality for clues.

ILFORD MYSTERY : TWO CHARGED

Frederick Bywaters was also charged over the murder of Percy Thompson.

Edith Thompson leaves the court under escort during her trial at Ilford. Both Thompson and Bywaters were found guilty and were executed in January 1923.

Winnie Ruth Judd

Winnie Ruth Judd was convicted of a double murder in 1932 and sentenced to death, but the ruling was not carried out as she was later declared insane.

Mrs. Winnie Ruth Judd, the doctor's wife and minister's daughter, wanted at Los Angeles. This picture was telephoned across America and cabled from New York by the "Daily Mirror's" Bartlane process, Western Union transmission.

Charlotte Bryant

In January 1936 Charlotte Bryant was accused of murdering her husband, Frederick John Bryant. It was alleged that she had administered poison over a substantial period and she was sentenced to hang for

Mrs. Swann and her daughter Valerie.

Carmen Swann

Carmen Swann, pictured with her daughter Valerie, who was found dead in February 1936. Carmen was found guilty of the eight-year-old's murder and sentenced to death, although she was reprieved within 24 hours as she was terminally ill with tuberculosis.

Margaret Allen

Margaret Allen was a lesbian who dressed in men's clothes and preferred to be called "Bill". On 29th August 1948 she battered her neighbour, Nancy Ellen Chadwick, who had come to borrow a cup of sugar, to death with a hammer. Allen confessed to the police that she was "in one of my funny moods" when she committed the murder.

Allen was found guilty and convicted on 8th December 1948 and sentenced to hang. Here, an official posts the notices of her execution on 12th January 1949.

THE LIFE OR DEATH ORDEALS OF MRS. CHRISTOFI

By HOWARD JOHNSON

Louisa Merrifield
The crowd queue up to read the two notices posted on the gate of Strangeways prison, Manchester, following the execution of Louisa Merrifield. There were no tears for Mrs Merrifield, who had been convicted of the murder of Sarah Ricketts in 1953.

Styllou Christofi
Styllou Christofi was found guilty of murdering her daughter-in-law and then burning her body in the back garden in 1954.

Ruth Ellis

Ruth Ellis, with racing driver boyfriend David Blakely, at the Little Club in London. Ellis was charged with murder after shooting Blakely in 1955.

Ruth Ellis posing beside David Blakely's car at Brands Hatch

Julie Yule was the chief witness for the prosecution in the Ruth Ellis trial. Her arm is in a sling due to a bullet wound in the hand fired by the murderess.

Mrs Van der Elst (left) and Mrs Pratt carry flowers into the prison, while Mrs Jacqueline Dyer carries petition papers in an attempt to have the sentence changed.

Crowds gathered outside Holloway prison the day Ruth Ellis was hanged. Little did they know that it would be the last time a woman would be hanged in Great Britain.

The front page of the *Daily Mirror* on 14th July 1955 questioned whether hanging should be abolished, following the execution of Ruth Ellis the previous day.

RUTH HORNBY
1926 ~ 1955

Ruth Ellis lies in a Buckinghamshire cemetery under her maiden name Ruth Hornby, not far from the place where David Blakely is buried.

The scene where Ruth Ellis shot her lover dead, at the Magdala public house in Hampstead. The bullet hole was still visible as a black spot below the window in 2003 when the Court of Appeal was asked to consider a pardon.

Myra Hindley
Myra Hindley became one of the most reviled women in
Britain for her part in the Moors murders that horrified the

Hindley's co-conspirator Ian Brady is driven away in the back of a police car.

HAVE YOU SEEN THIS BOY?

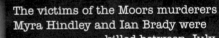

The victims of the Moors murderers Myra Hindley and Ian Brady were killed between July 1963 and October 1965. They were Pauline Reade, John Kilbride, Keith Bennett, Lesley Ann Downey and Edward Evans.

Police search under every rock and in every crevice for the victims' bodies on Saddleworth Moor in October 1965.

The newspaper headline announces that both Hindley and Brady have been found guilty and sentenced to life imprisonment.

Winifred Johnson, mother of Keith Bennett, conducts one of her many searches of Saddleworth Moor, with her son Ian (left) and a volunteer with metal detector (right) in August 1988.

DAILY Mirror

Saturday November 16 2002

NEWSPAPER OF THE YEAR 45p

MYRA DEAD

SEE PAGES 2,3,4,5,6 & 7

GONE BUT NOT FORGIVEN

MOORS murderer Myra Hindley died yesterday from respiratory failure. Her victims were, top from left, Edward Evans, 17, Lesley Ann Downey, 10, John Kilbride, 12, Keith Bennett, 12 and Pauline Reade, 16

MOORS MURDERER: 1942-2002

The *Daily Mirror* says goodbye and good riddance to Myra Hindley on the news of her death.

DAILY Mirror

Tuesday, May 18, 1993   COLOUR TV GUIDE: Pages 28 & 29   27p

SAIL TO FRANCE FREE — SEE PAGES 32 & 33

EXCLUSIVE: **Boy re-lives killer nurse ordeal**

I SURVIVED ANGEL OF DEATH'S POISON NEEDLE

A DEADLY COCKTAIL
MICHAEL'S medicine was spiked by Allitt.

'I remember it hurting.. then I started to scream'

By BILL DANIELS

BABY killer Beverley Allitt last night faced life behind bars - branded Britain's first woman mass murderer.

● DEADLIER THAN HINDLEY – Pages 2 & 3   ● A SEXLESS BULLY – Pages 4 & 5

● Turn to Page 3

Relatives in fury at £25,000 payout by State to Angel of Death who murdered four kids

DISGUSTING

Beverley Allitt
The front page of the *Daily Mirror* features Michael Davidson, whom nurse Beverley Allitt (inset), attempted to murder. Allitt, also pictured cuddling a baby, was found guilty of murdering four children in 1993.

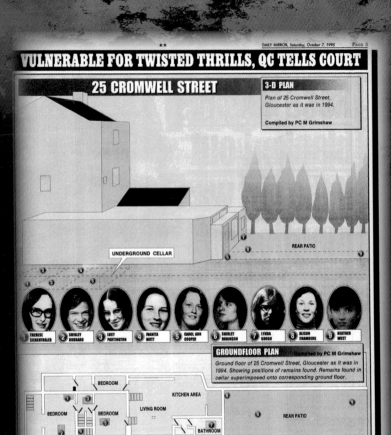

★★ DAILY MIRROR, Saturday, October 7, 1995 PAGE 3

VULNERABLE FOR TWISTED THRILLS, QC TELLS COURT

25 CROMWELL STREET

3-D PLAN

Plan of 25 Cromwell Street, Gloucester as it was in 1994.

Compiled by PC M Grimshaw

UNDERGROUND CELLAR

REAR PATIO

1 THERESE SIEGENTHALER
2 SHIRLEY HUBBARD
3 LUCY PARTINGTON
4 JUANITA MOTT
5 CAROL ANN COOPER
6 SHIRLEY ROBINSON
7 LYNDA GOUGH
8 ALISON CHAMBERS
9 HEATHER WEST

GROUNDFLOOR PLAN   Compiled by PC M Grimshaw

Ground floor of 25 Cromwell Street, Gloucester as it was in 1994. Showing positions of remains found. Remains found in cellar superimposed onto corresponding ground floor.

BEDROOM
KITCHEN AREA
BEDROOM   BEDROOM   LIVING ROOM
BATHROOM
REAR PATIO

was Lynda Gough, 19, who had been living at her home in Gloucester.

She occasionally lodged at Cromwell Street in 1972-3 and the skull was of elasticated cloth band.

Her body was found in what had been an inspection pit. Among the remains were tape, string and knotted fabric.

VICTIM No 3, it was claimed, was Carol Cooper, 15. She disappeared after her boyfriend put her on a bus in Worcester

in November, 1973. Her body was found with missing bones. The skull had been removed and legs dismembered. Around the skull was an elasticated cloth band.

VICTIM No 4, it was claimed, was university student Lucy Partington, 21.

She was never seen again after having a friend to catch a bus from Cheltenham in December, 1973.

Mr Leveson said: "This gentle girl must have been

picked up at the bus stop by the Wests operating in the way mentioned by Mrs Agius.

When her remains were found, the bones were jumbled, she had been decapitated and the hips had been disarticulated.

VICTIM No 5, it was claimed, was university student Lucy Partington, 21.

She was never seen again alive for whatever hideous purpose for some days.

VICTIM No 5, it was claimed, was Therese Siegenthaler, 21. She vanished while hitchhik-

ing in April, 1974. Her naked, dismembered body was found in front of a false fireplace.

VICTIM No 6, it was claimed was Shirley Robinson, 18. She ran away from home in November, 1974 and was never seen again. Her decapitated and legless body was found together with the remains of a gruesome mask fitted with breathing equipment.

VICTIM No 7, it was claimed,

was Juanita Mott, 18. After an unsettled family life she moved to Cromwell Street, and vanished in April, 1975.

She was the last person to be found in the cellar. It was full.

VICTIM No 8, it was claimed was Shirley Robinson, 18.

West had been having an affair with her at Cromwell Street. She was not among the abused and she was carrying his baby. She was the only vic-

tim to be found without any tape or rope with the body.

VICTIM No 9, it was claimed, was tearaway Alison Chambers, 17. A leather belt was found around her head.

VICTIM No 10, it was claimed, was Heather. She vanished in June, 1987. It was not known why she died. Perhaps, said Mr Leveson, she knew too much.

The case continues.

'FIRST AND LAST VICTIMS' – PAGES 4 & 5

pick them up and get them to lodge with us 9 –WHAT ROSE WEST ALLEGEDLY SAID

Rosemary West

This illustration shows the layout of the Wests' home and the position where nine of the girls' remains were found.

Rosemary West arrives at Winchester Crown Court in October 1995. The following month she was convicted of the murder of 10 girls.

A policeman carrying a box from the home of serial killers Rosemary and Fred West as 25 Cromwell Street, Gloucester, is searched in March 1994.

Tracie Andrews

Tracie Andrews is supported by Maureen Harvey, the mother of murdered Lee, and holds her hand at a police press conference in 1996. Andrews originally claimed a mystery road-rage attacker killed her boyfriend but later admitted to the crime.

house he shared with Hindley.

Meanwhile, Maureen Smith, Hindley's sister, claimed that the accused had become a "changed woman" after she met Brady. She had turned into a woman that hated babies, children and people in general. When Hindley was asked about the body found in the locked room of her home, she said: "I don't know, and I am not saying anything. My story is the same as Ian's." She also said: "I didn't do it. Ian did not do it. David Smith is a liar. I am saying nothing else until I have seen Ian."

When Mrs Downey came to give evidence, she stared at Hindley and Brady in the dock, and said between sobs: "I'll kill you … I'll kill you. An innocent baby." When told by Mr Mars-Jones to try not to distress herself, she said: "She sits there staring at me and she took a little baby's life, the beast." Mrs Downey told how she had been shown the photos of her daughter by police. Nine photos of Lesley had been found in one of the suitcases in the left luggage office. One tape recording was played in both closed proceedings and in open court. Mrs Downey had identified the child's voice on the recording as that of her daughter, Lesley. Hindley and Brady were also heard on the tape. Hindley and Brady were heard to speak in court for the first time on the 11th day of the hearing in the case. Both said they were not guilty of the charges against them. They were both sent for trial by magistrates, and their case would be heard the following year, in 1966. On 1st January 1966, it was claimed that the couple had requested permission to get married, but their request was denied. The trial date was announced as starting on 19th April, in Chester. Both had objected to the trial being held in Manchester due to "local prejudice". The day before the trial began the papers reported that all parties were ready. For the first time in many years, the Attorney General would lead for the Crown in a murder case. Sir Elwyn Jones, QC, would make the opening speech, which, it was suggested, could last as long as two days. It was expected that the trial would last four weeks. In his opening speech, in front of the jury and Mr Justice Fenton Atkinson, Sir Elwyn said that Hindley had pleaded not guilty to a fourth charge of harbouring Brady, but that this was the only alternative unless they charged her with John Kilbride's murder as well. It was Mr and Mrs Smith's call to Stalybridge police station on Thursday 7th October 1965 that had "unlocked" the case and led to the investigation which solved the mysteries he told the court. Both Smith and his wife had been desperate to get into the police car that arrived to collect them from the telephone kiosk on the Hattersley estate. They were both extremely frightened. Maureen Smith was the first witness to go into the witness box; she told the all-man jury about moorland trips with her sister and Brady. When David Smith gave evidence, he told the court that he had to wait outside until Hindley blinked the lights three times as a signal that it was alright for him to knock on the door and collect the wine bottles on the night that Edward Evans died. He said he "just froze" as he realized what Brady was doing to the teenager.

During the trial, police chiefs faced lengthy cross-examinations over their handling of interviews with the accused couple. For his part, Brady denied any knowledge of Lesley or John, but he did admit to having met with Edward. He also said that Hindley did what he told her to do. He told of his struggle with Edward, and, as before, even admitted to hitting him with an axe, but he also claimed that Smith had hit the teenager with a stick. He was questioned by his defence counsel, Mr Emlyn Hooson, QC.

Hindley was called to the witness box by her counsel, Mr Godfrey Heilpern, QC. She denied any part of the death of Edward Evans and any knowledge of the deaths and moorland burials of Lesley Ann Downey and 12-year-old John Kilbride. Talking of Edward she said she saw him lying on the floor in the living room and saw David Smith kicking the boy and jabbing at him with a stick. Asked how she felt about seeing what was happening to Edward she said: "I was sick. I was crying. I was horrified. I was frightened." Later in her evidence, Hindley spoke of the time – Boxing Day night in 1964 – when Brady was preparing to take photographs of a girl that she now knew to be Lesley Downey. "The girl was very frightened and crying," said the accused woman in the box. She went on: "I was frightened someone would hear. As soon as she started crying, I started to panic. I was worried. That is why I was so brusque and cruel in my attitude. I just wanted her to be quiet." In her evidence, Hindley alleged that Lesley Ann, as the young child was referred to in court, was brought to the house by David Smith and another man – and taken away again after the photographs. Asked about her feelings when she heard a tape recording played in court and read the transcript, Hindley replied: "I am ashamed." She added that there was some argument because she told Brady she did not want him to take photographs of the girl. Cross-examined by the Attorney General, the accused said she put her hands over her ears when Brady was grappling with Edward Evans. However, she told the court that she did not put her hands over her ears as Lesley Ann screamed during her ordeal. When asked why not, she confirmed that she had wanted the child to be quiet. She was also asked by the Attorney General why she did not get the little girl out of the situation. Hindley replied: "I should have done that but I didn't. I have no defence for that. No defence. It was indefensible. I was cruel. And pitiless. I was cruel." Questioned about the disposal plan for Edward's body she claimed that Brady and Smith discussed it and she was not consulted. She added: "I would have done anything as long as Ian did not get into trouble." On 4th May 1966, Sir Elwyn Jones described Hindley as a "calculated, pretty cool co-operator in murder". She had formed an "evil partnership" with Brady he told the trial jury in his closing speech. He also mentioned that eight "trademarks" of murder linked the deaths of Edward, John and Lesley Ann. But Emlyn Hooson said that before the jury could convict on any of the three murder charges, jurors had to be sure there was proof. The following day, Mr Justice Fenton Atkinson began his summing-up to the jury in the final stages of the trial. Surveying the evidence in the three murder charges against the accused, the judge told the jury: "I suppose hearing such allegations, reading about such allegations, the first reaction of kindly, charitable people is to say 'this is so terrible that anyone doing anything like that must be mentally afflicted'. You have to put that aside at once. From first to last in this case, there has not been the smallest suggestion that either of these two is mentally abnormal or that they are not fully and completely responsible for their actions. If – and I must underline the word if – what the prosecution say is right, you are dealing here, are you not, with two sadistic killers of the utmost depravity. Normal people would say, 'could anyone be as wicked as that?' That was what the prosecution were setting out to prove."

On 6th May 1966, "partners in murder" Hindley and Brady were jailed for life at the end of the "Bodies on the Moors" trial. The jury took just two hours and 14 minutes to decide that Brady was guilty of the murders of Edward, Lesley Ann and John. Hindley was found guilty of the murders of Edward and Lesley Ann, but not of John; however, she was found guilty of harbouring Brady knowing that he had killed the child. After the jury's verdicts, the judge said: "Ian Brady, these were three calculated, cruel, cold-blooded murders." He added: "In your case I pass the only sentence which the law now allows, which is three concurrent sentences of life imprisonment." An impassive Brady then left the dock. Hindley remained. The judge said to her: "In your case, Hindley, you have been found guilty by the jury of two equally horrible murders and, to the third, as an accessory after the fact of murder. On the two murders, the sentence is two concurrent life sentences of life imprisonment. On the accessory charge, a concurrent sentence of seven years' imprisonment." As she was sentenced, Hindley swayed forward and looked down. Then she left the dock. Later, both convicted murderers were escorted from the court building to a police van. As the van swung out from the Chester Castle courtyard, a crowd of about 250 people pressed forward and there were boos and cheers. The couple were then taken to a remand centre. Meanwhile there was tremendous praise for the police who had solved the cases. The following day it was reported that talks would take place between police forces concerned with searching for traces of vanished children on Saddleworth Moor. Detectives believed that at least two more children were buried on the moor, including Keith Bennett and Pauline Reade. In October 1966 Hindley's final appeal failed. She had been given special permission to leave Holloway prison in London to attend the Court of Appeal. She appealed against the conviction on the ground that Mr Justice Fenton Atkinson had erred in not granting separate trials for the two accused. In November 1966, it was suggested that there was a possibility that the murderers might help police when it was announced that CID looking for Keith and Pauline would question them. In January the following year, the murderers were finally questioned about the two missing children. Two of the three detectives that visited both Brady and Hindley were involved in the original inquiry. The couple were not often mentioned in the press again until September 1972 when a new storm blew up over plans for the killers to be allowed a reunion. Meanwhile, it was revealed that, due to special treatment, Hindley had become known as the "queen of Holloway". There had already been anger that the governor had permitted her to walk outside the prison earlier that month, but the books she was allowed and her alleged carpeted cell were causing discontent among other inmates at the women's prison in north London. Fourteen months later, Hindley was back in the press when she appeared in court in January 1974 accused of a part in an alleged jailbreak plot. She was charged along with another prisoner at London's Old Street Court, while a woman officer at Holloway was on bail charged with conspiring to effect an escape. Hindley was then sent for trial at the Old Bailey the following month for the escape plot, alongside 22-year-old Maxine Croft and the prison officer, 29-year-old Patricia Cairns. The court heard how Hindley's "close link" to Cairns had gone unheeded. Their love affair had been revealed and reported to the authorities by another woman prisoner, who, when no evidence was found, was sentenced to lose 180 days' remission. As no one believed her Hindley and Cairns were free to plan the escape. At the Old Bailey, Cairns received six years in jail for her part, while Hindley received a token 12 months behind bars. For acting as their go-between, Maxine Croft received 18 months. Soon after, Hindley had a letter smuggled out of prison saying that unless her female lover was released, she wanted to stay in jail. However, all that changed four years later when she made a "sensational" plea for freedom. In November 1978 she wrote a 20,000-word document to the Home Secretary requesting parole. She argued that she had been wrongly convicted. Home Secretary Merlyn Rees asked for the case to be considered by a committee of three parole board members and two Home Office representatives. However, her earlier statement would be edited because it was felt that the joint committee should not consider her wrongful conviction argument.

Less than 10 years later, in July 1984, the convicted murderer was boasting in jail that she would be freed within months. She also made astonishing claims that VIP treatment would be laid on for her – including a plane. By now in Cookham Wood jail, she said: "I won't be here much longer. This is the end of the line for me." She claimed that she would be escorted to an airfield where she would take a private plane out of Britain. She claimed that she would start a new life abroad, somewhere that she hadn't been heard of, where she could change her life and live anonymously. However, she was hated by other inmates who declared that hanging was too good for "Mad Myra", as she had become known. As hindsight has shown, Hindley was wrong, and more than two years later, in November 1986, it was reported that she had broken her 21-year silence in order to tell detectives "the grim secrets of the moors". Her disclosures from prison launched a new search of Saddleworth Moor. She said she had decided to speak out after receiving a letter from Winnie Johnson, mother of missing Keith. In a statement she said: "I received a letter, the first ever, from the mother of one of the missing children, and this has caused me enormous distress. I have agreed to help the Manchester police in any way possible, and have today identified from photographs and maps places that I know were of particular interest to Ian Brady, some of which I visited with him. I have searched my heart and memory and given whatever help I can give to the police. I hope that one day people will be able to forgive the wrong I have done, and know the truth of what I have not done. But for now I want the police to be able to conclude their inquiries so ending public speculation and the private anguish of those directly involved."

For 20 years the couple had remained silent about the truth of what happened to Keith and Pauline, but then Brady confessed to the *Sunday People* that they had both been murdered, backing Hindley's story about the two children in a twist that came to light in 1986. Later that same month, on the bleak wastes of the "murder moors", police pegged out the site where they would begin attempting to solve the mystery of the two lost children. A handful of traffic cones marked the desolate acres around Wildcat Quarry where the search would begin. Meanwhile, police were banned from offering Brady and Hindley a no-charge deal in return for them confessing their secrets. The Director of Public Prosecutions said no because he believed such immunity would anger the public. The couple, it was reported, could face fresh charges if police did find more bodies buried on Saddleworth Moor. On 20th November 1986, the anguished brother of victim Pauline Reade pleaded with Hindley to tell him the truth about his sister's fate. Paul Reade watched as police began searching the storm-lashed moors. He said: "I need to know in detail what happened to her. I need to know how she suffered." On the freezing moors near Oldham, the searchers and their eight dogs found only animal remains. The detective in charge, Peter Topping, said: "The weather has not been kind to us. In the space of a few hours we have experienced all four seasons. But we plan to be here for quite a while." Meanwhile, Winifred Johnson, Keith's mother, waited at her Manchester home. Fighting back her tears, she said: "I know deep in my heart that there will be a knock on the door. Probably not today or tomorrow ... but sometime soon." Paul Reade said: "There is nothing for Hindley to hide anymore. But I need to know in detail what happened to Pauline ... was she beaten about the head like Edward Evans or did they torture her like little Lesley Ann Downey?" It was what kept Paul awake at night. It was what had been haunting him for 23 years. The macabre crimes had blighted so many families. Both Winnie and Joan suffered from stress-related illnesses. For many years, Joan Reade could not come to terms with her daughter's death. In other news, it was reported that the renewed search for bodies had caused Brady, who by then had been transferred to Park Lane Hospital on Merseyside, to suffer from depression.

For years, Joan Reade had hoped her daughter would return home. For years, she used to walk the streets at night, searching, hoping ... just in case. Often she would run after a bus if she saw a passenger with long brown hair like Pauline's. The Reade children had grown up in a close-knit Manchester community: rows of two-up and two-down houses, where doors were always open and children played happily in the street. One of those children had been Hindley. Paul Reade remembered her saying that they had grown up with the same crowd. He said: "It's hard for me to explain, but there was something different about Myra compared to the other kids. I never thought anything of it at the time, but when our Pauline disappeared all the neighbours rallied round but Myra never called in to see how we were coping. We hardly knew Brady. He was only around our area for about a year, and even then I can't remember seeing his face because he used to wear his motorcycle helmet with a scarf over his face all the time."

Finally, towards the end of November 1986, Brady agreed to help the police with their new searches. He was furious that Hindley had spoken to police, and he sent her a clear message to watch what she said – or face having her deepest secrets about the unsolved murders exposed. He reminded her that he had kept six letters she wrote to him when they were lovers. The following month it was revealed that Hindley was close to "cracking up" after being quizzed for the fifth time by police. Later that same month she asked for more time to "help in the hunt" for the two buried children. "Give me a day more," she shouted at her Home Office "minder" as darkness began to fall on Saddleworth Moor. During a seven-hour visit she had been trying to aid police in finding the graves. During the search she told the official that she would not seek parole when her case came up for review in 1990. However, her trip was confined to one day only. Nevertheless, at the end of March 1987 Hindley was back on the moor, where she was guarded by armed police. Early in April that year, she finally told police how she helped to kill Keith and Pauline. Her confession came after a four-day grilling. She also then revealed the roles she and Brady had played in the sadistic murders of the three other children. She finally admitted that she and Brady lured youngsters to the moors by inviting them on picnics and to search for missing gloves. Only hours after the *Mirror* revealed that she had given full details to police, Hindley put out a statement through her solicitor confirming the story. She said she had decided she could no longer live a lie. Hindley declared: "I admit my role in these awful events … I consider myself to be as guilty as my former lover, Ian Brady, although our roles were different." Now, at least, the families of Keith and Pauline knew that their loved ones were buried on Saddleworth Moor. Hindley's statement continued with reasons why, for so many years, she hid the truth. "I was still obsessed and infatuated with Ian Brady. I could not bring myself to admit the truth about our crimes … I did what I could to hide the truth from myself and from others, believing this was the only way I could survive the ordeal of a very long prison sentence … Throughout my sentence, I have been haunted by the continued suffering of the relatives of the two children that were missing at the time of my arrest. Until recently, I have been utterly overwhelmed by the numerous difficulties of revealing the truth. I have had to consider the consequences for my family, who have suffered far more than I have. And I have been fearful of the effect that facing up to the truth would have on me and my existence in prison, which has always been a tremendous ordeal … I received a letter from Mrs Johnson begging for help." In June 1987, Hindley made a "dramatic" plea to Brady to help. It was triggered by a second letter from Winnie. In July 1987, a child's body was found on Saddleworth Moor. The grim discovery was made on the bleak moor where, for seven months, police had been searching. The body was found in a three-foot peat grave 100 yards from the spot where Lesley Ann's body had been discovered. A stretcher was used to gently carry the body into a windowless police van. Both Pauline and Keith had been killed by the sex murderers during summer picnics on the moor. The body was identified as that of Pauline Reade. In October 1987, Hindley wrote to Mrs Ann West, Lesley Ann's mother, of her "monstrous evil". She wrote: "Dear Mrs West, Thank you for your letter, and I'm sorry it has taken me so long to reply to it. I think I know how difficult it must have been to write to me, and this reply is going to be even more difficult, because I find it almost impossible to express the way I feel about the indescribable suffering I have caused you, your family and the other families concerned … I was evil, and I make no excuses whatsoever for my part in any of the past. The letter from Mrs Johnson last October absolutely devastated me, and made me realise finally that I could no longer remain silent, whatever the cost to my family or myself." The letter continued: "But please believe me – not for my sake, but simply in the hope that it will give you even a little peace of mind, that however monstrous and unforgiveable the crime was, your child was not tortured to death." After analysis of the letter by an expert, Hindley was branded a liar "who sheds nothing but crocodile tears for her victims". Leading psychologists agreed that Hindley felt sorry for no one but herself.

Handwriting analyst Jillie Collings said: "There isn't a genuine or sincere word of concern about what she had done." And top psychiatrist Dr Richard Badcock believed the letter did not have the ring of truth. "She might be trying to change the public view of her as evil," he said. Despite the admissions of killing Pauline and the discovery of her body, the Director of Public Prosecutions decided not to put the murderers on trial again, but the families of the victims were outraged by that decision, which was made at the beginning of 1988. In April that year Pauline's devastated family were at the inquest into how the young girl died. She had been slashed across the throat, twice. Pauline's gold and pink dress and underskirt had been pulled up to the waist. Her knickers were missing. Photographs taken at the post-mortem showed a four-inch slash across her throat, which was so savage it almost split the spinal column. The jury at the inquest took less than five minutes to conclude that Pauline Reade had been unlawfully killed.

Police chief Peter Topping took early retirement in June 1988. He had worked tirelessly to search for the bodies of the missing children. The following year, as students of the Open University quit when Hindley was awarded a degree in humanities by the institution, the *Mirror* readers voted overwhelmingly that Hindley hadn't changed a bit. More than 28,200 voted she was still evil and not "a very gentle person with normal loving, caring feelings". Just under 1,000 readers disagreed, believing she had changed. Brady's opinion followed the majority. In 1990, Brady claimed that Hindley had been the one who chose their victims and strangled

Lesley Ann. On 30th January he finally revealed the sinister secrets of the child killings that shocked the world. In a chilling letter, he told how Hindley strangled the child with a silk cord, then enjoyed toying with the weapon in public. Brady painted a portrait of a sadistic woman killer, who personally picked victims and treated the murders as a bizarre "substitute marriage ritual". He launched a bitter attack on his former lover's "pack of lies", and her "sanctimonious sham concern for the relatives of the victims". And he poured scorn on claims that she was reformed. He gave a horrifying account of Lesley Ann's murder by Hindley. He wrote: "She insisted upon killing Lesley Ann Downey with her own hands using a two-foot length of silk cord." Brady said that injuries to the nose and forehead of one victim were inflicted by Hindley, who also took part in lesbian assaults on victims. But Hindley bluntly denied she played the dominant role in the murders. However, in December 1995, she did admit that she was more culpable than her accomplice, Brady. Despite fighting over the years for her freedom, she eventually heard in February 1997 that she would never be freed when the Home Secretary, Michael Howard, backed a 1990 decision that she should serve a "whole life" term. Jack Straw, the Home Secretary in July that year, gave her no sympathy either. In November 1998 she was told she could expect to die in jail. Her child victims had met a brutal end, but Hindley died peacefully in November 2002, in a hospital room with a priest by her side. Her solicitor Taylor Nichol said: "Myra was deeply aware of the terrible crimes she had committed and of the suffering caused to those who died and to their relatives. She was acutely aware that she would not be forgiven by many."

In June 2013, Brady described his killings as "petty compared to politicians and soldiers", a forensic psychiatrist revealed. Brady was seen in public for the first time in nearly 50 years as he launched a bid to be allowed to die in prison. As the judge opened a mental health tribunal at Ashworth special hospital on Merseyside – where the serial killer was held – he spoke in a barely audible Glasgow mumble of "precedence" and "medical witnesses".

The child killer, by this time 75, had been force-fed for more than a decade after going on hunger strike in protest at his treatment in a secure mental hospital.

Brady mumbled as he spoke to the judge and appeared to be making notes off-screen with his right hand as his bid to be sent back to prison began. Dr Cameron Boyd, a forensic psychiatrist, who is the medical member of the tribunal's panel, said: "I asked if he wanted to die. He refused to answer that question.

"I asked about previous behaviour that might be seen as abnormal, regarding to his offences.

"He said it was an existential exercise, personal philosophy and interpretation and in some way his behaviour was petty compared to politicians and soldiers in relation to wars." The mental health tribunal itself took place behind closed doors at Ashworth Hospital on Merseyside. But proceedings were being relayed by video to press and relatives of Brady and Hindley's victims at a court 40 miles away in Manchester. Brady, wearing gold-framed dark-tinted glasses he rarely removed, sat hunched over a four-inch-thick pile of psychiatric reports – details picked out in purple highlighter pen. The end of the feeding tube that has kept him alive during a 13-year hunger strike, fastened to his right cheek with white surgical tape, swung as he lunged forward, scribbling furiously. He looked dishevelled, his skin yellowing. A three-inch hump on his back betrayed a degenerative spinal medical condition, spondylitis.

Brady lifted documents from a ring binder closer to his eyes trying to focus on the writing. He constantly whispered and passed notes to his solicitor – jabbing at them with his pen. Lawyer Corinne Singer was forced to raise her finger to her mouth several times to urge him to keep quiet. Forty-nine years and one day to the day of the hearing, 12-year-old Keith Bennett vanished on the way to his grandmother's house. His mum Winnie waved him off after seeing him safely across a level crossing near their home in Manchester. His body has never been found.

Outside the Manchester court building where the tribunal was being relayed via a video link, relatives handed out flyers, which read: "Keith was deprived of the life that he should have led and all that he could have been."

Brady's barrister Nathalie Lieven, QC, started his case with evidence from forensic psychiatrist Dr Adrian Grounds. He said that Brady had been sent to Ashworth in 1995 after 19 years in prison after a "significant deterioration" in his condition and he was diagnosed as having a psychotic illness, but the killer said he was "acting". Dr Grounds said in Brady's early years in Ashworth he had "hallucinations and paranoid delusional beliefs" and thought that his thoughts were being interfered with. But his condition improved over the next 10 years with the help of anti-psychotic drugs and his psychotic symptoms were "considerably less". Brady had last had anti-psychotic medication 10 years before, and Dr Grounds said he believed he could no longer be classed as mentally ill although he still had a personality disorder described as "paranoid narcissistic".

"Characterised by superiority, self-centredness, contempt, hostility," he added. The tribunal was scheduled to last around a week and had been postponed from June the previous year, when Brady fell ill after suffering a seizure. It was not known if Brady himself would give evidence.

Winnie died aged 78, on 18th August in 2012, without being able to fulfil her last wish of giving her son a proper burial.

Judge Robert Atherton told the hearing: "There will be no questions about the likely place of the body of Keith Bennett. The reason we shall not be making these inquiries is they are not relevant to the issues we have to decide. The whereabouts of Keith Bennett's body is not a matter we have authority to inquire about." The solicitor who represented Keith's mother Winnie said: "Sadly I have given up hope that Brady will reveal the whereabouts of Keith's body."

Brady has, all his life, been a control fanatic. He controlled his victims. Now, near his end, he wants to control the authorities, the newspapers quoted. "It is a great insult to his victims and very distressing to their families if we allow him to do that. We should not give him that privilege."

Members of a group, backed by Keith's brother Alan, who want Greater Manchester Police to reopen their search, attended the hearing to hand out leaflets in support of their aim. Alan, 53, had called for a "calm, controlled, peaceful and respectful" protest. He added: "I have been advised by those concerned that I should not expect anything from this hearing, it is about Brady and not Keith. So thanks to all concerned for giving Keith a voice outside the hearing while Brady has his say inside. It is no longer all about Brady."

Another brother of Keith's, Terry, said: "Why should he have the right to a hearing? He should be left where he is."

Beverley Allitt

1991

On 17th June 1991, the *Mirror* stated: "Four babies all under a year old may have been killed with drug overdoses in a hospital children's ward." Detectives feared that 10 other babies and youngsters, who survived heart attacks and breathing difficulties, had also been poisoned with the same drug. A 22-year-old nurse from the ward had been given extended leave it was reported. The children all fell ill between January and May 1991 and the hospital called in detectives after tests on one boy who survived revealed an unusual amount of insulin in his bloodstream. Insulin is known to be absorbed quickly by the body and leaves no trace. The children were all patients in Ward Four at Grantham's District General Hospital in Lincolnshire. Every member of the nursing staff had been questioned. The father of the nurse given extended leave said: "I know nothing about her being questioned by police. She is a dedicated nurse. It is her whole life." At the time, medical experts were examining the records of every patient in the ward in the previous few months. They also talked to older children who were patients in the ward, along with their parents. Detective Superintendent Stuart Clifton said: "I can't say yet if there is anything sinister." One of the problems that police faced was that the babies who died were cremated. Staff at the Lincolnshire hospital became concerned earlier in 1991 at the high number of toddlers having cardiac or respiratory arrests. However, they expected to find a normal explanation. They hadn't bargained on the shocks to come such as the insulin traces that were found during a blood test, and hospital chiefs called the police. Ward Four had 20 beds and treated children from a few weeks old up to the age of 11. A senior hospital official said: "It may well be that the inquiry will reveal nothing untoward. This is a traumatic situation and particularly dreadful for those involved in the inquiry. Our nursing staff on the ward are dedicated and we feel for them." He added: "We want to assure parents their children will receive a high standard of care here." One child who survived after collapsing in Ward Four was five-year-old Brad Gibson. He suffered a heart attack a day after being admitted with pneumonia. Doctors and nurses in the ward fought for 32 minutes to revive him. His mother, Judith, 36, said: "Police told me they are investigating the possible misuse of drugs. We couldn't understand why Brad collapsed. He was not seriously ill. But suddenly his heart gave out."

Four days later, the *Mirror* released a picture of "chubby-faced" ward nurse, Beverley Allitt – who was charged on 21st November 1991 with killing three babies and an 11-year-old boy. Allitt was led into court covered in a blanket as police struggled to hold back a furious crowd of parents screaming "Murderer!" The nurse was also accused of attempting to murder eight other youngsters, although she denied all charges. Weeping parents screamed abuse at the nurse as she was led into court to face charges of killing their babies. Shouts rang out as the stocky nurse was ushered before magistrates to be accused of the murders, attempted murders and of causing grievous bodily harm. The children's parents packed the tiny courtroom in Grantham for the five-minute hearing.

They sobbed and hugged each other as blonde Allitt was remanded in custody for her own safety. Allitt, who sat throughout the hearing with her hands in the pockets of her black jeans, had worked at the hospital for a year after completing her training. She was alleged to have murdered Liam Taylor, aged seven weeks, Becky Phillips, two months, Claire Peck, 15 months, and 11-year-old Timothy Hardwick. The attempted murder charges related to children ranging from one-month-old babies to a five-year-old boy. One of these children was Becky's twin sister Katie. Allitt's arrest followed a five-month investigation by a special squad of detectives and an emotional plea for swift action from the parents. Police believed throughout their investigations that two drugs had been used – both of which were potentially lethal. The children who had survived the attacks had all needed treatment in intensive care. Reporting restrictions were lifted at the hearing at the request of Allitt's solicitor, John Kendall. He said the nurse, who shared her parents' home near Grantham, wanted to make it clear she denied all the charges, "and will fight them through the courts at the appropriate time". Meanwhile, the manager of Grantham Hospital, Martin Gibson, said: "We are shocked and saddened that a former member of staff has been charged with causing the death of a number of children", while the children's parents stated that they would be suing South Lincolnshire health chiefs regardless of the case's outcome. The *Mirror* printed a picture of baby Liam Taylor nestled in his father's arms just days before his mystery death. He now appeared on a court list as the youngest child alleged to have been murdered by Beverley Allitt. Liam's mother, Joanne, 25, sobbed uncontrollably in court, while father Chris said: "We are just numbed by the whole affair. For a healthy baby to be taken away from you like this is something you can't explain."

On 11th March 1992, three more other murder attempts were added to the charges against Allitt. Detectives put the new charges to her at New Hall prison in West Yorkshire, where she was being held on remand. They alleged that she tried to kill Jonathan Jobson, 16, of Peterborough, Dorothy Lowe, 79, a resident of a nursing home in Leicestershire, and Michael Davidson, 11, a patient at Grantham Hospital. The nurse from Corby Glen was due to appear before magistrates the following week, where police were expected to ask for her to be committed for trial on all charges. In August that same year the former nurse was moved to Rampton top-security hospital, where it was reported that she needed sustained medical treatment. The following year, in February 1993, it was the nurses' rota that gave police chilling clues to mass murder, the court heard. It showed a common link in the deaths of the four children on Ward Four. Allitt was always on duty when children were struck down by heart attacks. The four children that died and the nine others that were attacked had all been injected with insulin or suffocated, it was claimed. The baffling string of deaths and dramatic collapses came after Allitt was rejected for a permanent job at Grantham District Hospital. When police studied the rotas, it became clear that there was a grim pattern. Prosecutor John Goldring told Nottingham Crown Court: "Nurse Allitt had been present at each of the 24 attacks thought to have taken place on patients." The next nurse on the list had been present 10 times. Allitt looked pale and haggard as she sat in the dock listening to the case unfold.

Since her arrest, she had reportedly suffered from anorexia nervosa and her weight plummeted from 13 stone to seven. She continued to deny murdering four children and attempting to murder nine others, and she denied all other charges against her. She had finished her training at the hospital in February 1991 but wasn't offered a permanent position. Instead, she got a temporary post, just prior to the attacks. Liam Taylor died on 23rd February 1991. He had a chest infection and Allitt was told to nurse him. One evening, after he was fed, he was violently sick. No one else on the ward was aware of that, stated the prosecutor. "For much of that evening and the night the defendant was alone with Liam." Two alarms were attached to the baby's body, but failed to go off. When his condition deteriorated, Allitt told another nurse: "Oh, look at him. He has gone a funny colour." The tiny baby then suffered a heart attack and later died. Timothy Hardwick, 11, died of a heart attack on 5th March. "Something was done to him," said Goldring. "We cannot say what. Sensibly, there is only one candidate." Police were called and began looking at the case of five-month-old Paul Crampton. Paul, who survived three heart attacks, was found to have been injected with a massive dose of insulin. "Incredible though it may seem, it was clear there was a criminal at large on Ward Four," said the prosecutor. Among the records checked was a notebook giving details of patients. It was kept by nurses on the ward, but it had been tampered with. "Someone who didn't want the police to see what was in the book had taken a pair of scissors and cut out a number of pages," continued Goldring. "What did it mean?" It meant that the criminal had access to the book and knew that each collapse in the ward was to be looked at again. Later, another notebook disappeared, which showed which nurses dealt with particular patients. When Allitt was arrested, it was found in a bag in a wardrobe at her home.

At Allitt's trial, the jury was told that the decision of the hospital to call the police was "unprecedented". It was soon clear that this wasn't a medical inquiry and the deaths were obviously the work of a criminal. All the nurse's explanations to police were "wholly unconvincing". The prosecution said: "We cannot say in each case exactly what the defendant did to a particular child. No one was watching her. In some cases she injected insulin. In other cases she gave another drug or a mixture of drugs. In some she may simply have placed her hand over a baby's mouth or nose, interfering with the oxygen supply with dramatic consequences for a child who was ill." The motive at this point remained a mystery. "Why should a nurse do these things?" he asked. Toddler Kayley Desmond was not seriously ill when she was admitted to Grantham Hospital with a chest infection, but the 15-month-old's condition worsened one night when Allitt was on duty, the jury was told. Her face and body became mottled and she stopped breathing. She later recovered, but a "remarkable" discovery was made when X-ray plates were checked – there was an air bubble under her right armpit. "Someone took a syringe and deliberately injected Kayley under the armpit," claimed Goldring.

On 17th February 1993, a young father choked back tears at the trial as he recalled the tragic last hours of his baby son. Chris Taylor, father of Liam, the first victim, told the jury that only hours before his son suffered a massive heart attack he had believed his sick child was getting better. His voice breaking with emotion, he said that he had seen his son open his eyes and reach out for his teddy bear. However, in the early hours of the following morning, as he and his wife snatched a few hours' sleep for the first time in two nights, they were woken with the news that their son had taken a turn for the worse. He nodded and whispered "yes" when the court was told Liam suffered a cardiac arrest. That morning the tiny child was christened. He died later that afternoon. The court was told that Liam was the first of the four young victims to die on Ward Four. Allitt, her eyes downcast, sat in the dock and avoided looking at the young father as he struggled with his emotions. Meanwhile, the judge, Mr Justice Latham, said: "It is important that we do not expose the families to any more trauma than is absolutely necessary." The trial was suddenly postponed on 10th March 1993 as new information emerged. Then, a few days later, came fears that the trial might be stopped altogether after it was reported that

Allitt was suffering from the consequences of severe anorexia. On 25th March, however, it transpired that Allitt had also been seen wrongly injecting an elderly patient who later collapsed. Auxiliary Alice Stewart said she checked diabetic Dorothy Lowe in the early hours. She told Nottingham Crown Court: "I found Beverley injecting Dot. She put the syringe in her pocket, which I thought odd. She looked shocked seeing me." Soon afterwards, Mrs Lowe became "unrousable". Robert Jennings, then deputy manager at the home in Waltham on the Wolds, said Dorothy had not been due an injection. Branded by the newspapers as "evil", Beverley Allitt was convicted on 13th May 1993 of murdering two babies treated on Ward Four. She was found guilty of murdering Becky Phillips and Claire Peck with massive drug overdoses. She was also found guilty of attacking three other children, but the jury had yet to reach a verdict about the two other deaths. Allitt was not in the dock when she was branded a double killer as she was being given treatment at Rampton secure hospital for her illness. The court heard that Becky had been taken to hospital alongside her twin sister to be treated for a stomach infection. Allitt gave her a dose of insulin. Her parents were later told she was well enough to go home, but four hours after leaving hospital she died – after giving a pitiful scream. Claire was injected with potassium. She turned blue, arched her back and stopped breathing. She recovered, but had a fatal attack soon after being left alone with the murdering Allitt. While Allitt was cleared of trying to murder Kayley Desmond, two-year-old Henry Chan and five-week-old Christopher King, she was convicted of causing them grievous bodily harm.

Facing a life behind bars, Allitt was branded Britain's first woman serial killer. One of the youngsters she tried to kill told for the first time how he was saved by his screams as his heart stopped. Eleven-year-old Michael Davidson's piercing cry echoed around Ward Four, halting a deadly injection of potassium. "I remember the needle hurting straight away and I started to scream. I was just lying there screaming. The next thing I remember is being connected to all sorts of machines." Michael gave his account of what happened to him as Allitt was finally convicted of the series of crimes that shocked the nation. Parents of her tiny victims cheered and wept when the jury at Nottingham Crown Court finally found her guilty of murder number four, and of the attack on Michael and two other youngsters. Alan Davidson, Michael's father, declared: "She is a sick monster and must never be allowed to put anyone else at risk." The jury had reached its final verdicts following a six-day session. Allitt still wasn't in court. She was confined to Rampton top-security hospital where she'd spent most of the three-month trial. Joanna Hunt, whose baby daughter became sick twice after being nursed by Allitt, was convinced that her child was lucky to survive. It was also reported that the jurors were to receive stress counselling following the harrowing case.

Michael Davidson described how he'd been struggling to rebuild his life after the former nurse had given him so much poison that his heart stopped. It was only the quick thinking of a doctor thumping on his chest that brought him "back to life". He had been treated for simple stomach injuries when Allitt struck, and he was left with violent mood swings that almost led to him being expelled from school for attacking his teachers and classmates. He said: "I have had a lot of bad dreams and I go sleepwalking. Sometimes I dream that someone is trying to throw me out of a window. I like going to school, but I know that I can be very naughty. It is just something that happens. I lose my temper sometimes because there seems so much work to do. I lash out at people. Some days I forget my letters and I can't read or write properly and I get very upset." Michael had a counsellor to help him through his horrific ordeal, who made him feel better. The shattered parents of other victims were also trying to come to terms with their tragedies. Peter and Sue Phillips, parents of Becky, had lost one daughter and were facing life with her twin sister, Katie, who had been brain damaged by the ordeal. While Allitt was awaiting trial, Peter said: "They should bring back the rope for this woman. She should not be allowed to live. I want her to suffer the way we have suffered." The parents of murdered Timothy Hardwick couldn't bear to attend the trial. His mother Helen, who was dying of cancer, told friends that people looked to hospitals as places where people's health was repaired, not destroyed. Meanwhile Claire's mum, Sue Peck, told how she had had another baby daughter, but couldn't bear to be treated at Grantham during her pregnancy.

Allitt's murder spree was the greatest by a woman in modern times. It was surpassed only by Victorian woman Mary Ann Cotton, who was hanged in Durham after poisoning more than 20 people, including children, husbands, lovers and her mother between 1866 and 1872. A detective said: "Allitt's crimes are unprecedented in Britain." Her cool, confident attitude stunned police when they first quizzed her. She barely batted an eyelid when they charged her with murder. The man who headed the investigation, Stuart Clifton, said the killer's relaxed manner took them aback because she was only 22 years old and hadn't been in trouble before. But it transpired that Allitt had craved success as the "heroine" of the children's wards – and when that dream faded she launched a murder spree that was cited in the press as "more deadly than the crimes of Myra Hindley". Understandably, parents had trusted the care of their children to the cheerful young nurse, because they had no way of knowing that behind the smiling mask Allitt was callously scheming to take young lives. So what did turn Bev Allitt, a plain, ordinary woman whose ruthless ambition far outweighed her modest ability into Britain's first modern-day serial killer?

In the Lincolnshire village of Corby Glen where she was brought up, Allitt was remembered as a girl who loved children and was always in demand for babysitting. But there were early signs of the mental instability that would follow. In the four years between 1987 and 1991, Allitt was treated at Grantham District Hospital 24 times for injuries to her hands, legs, back and head. Medical staff suspected they were all self-inflicted. In one year alone, while training to be a nurse, she had 94 days off sick. Allitt's barrister told the court that senior hospital staff were informed of her problems ... but did nothing about it. The QC added: "It is a tragedy for everyone." Old schoolmates knew the nurse was "disturbed", and one of her former best friends, Rachel Oliver, said she was always drawing attention to herself. She was diagnosed with a rare form of Münchausen's Syndrome – a craving for attention, usually by inventing illnesses or through self-inflicted injury. In the most severe cases, sufferers attack others, often their own children. Detectives believed that the rejection Allitt felt when she failed to secure a permanent job after scraping through her final exams is what tipped her over the edge. She had been the only student nurse on the course at Grantham not to be offered a full-time job. She was also rejected for further training at another hospital. Through the weeks of turmoil at the hospital, caused by her murders, Allitt played the bustling "supernurse", raising the alarm and helping the emergency medical teams. While medical staff became more and more distressed at the chaos and tragedy on Ward Four, Allitt revelled in the attention she was getting. Colleagues rallied to support her. One said: "It seems crazy now, but everyone used to feel sorry for Bev. She was always in the thick of things." The 59 pages cut and torn from an exercise book finally convinced detectives that Allitt was the killer. Found in her bedroom, the pages pinpointed the movements of nursing staff and covered the 59 days when children were attacked. Police also discovered that a startling blueprint for murder also hit the bookshelves in Britain the year before Allitt first killed. The paperback, *The Death Shift*, told the story of 32-year-old Texas nurse, Genene Jones, jailed for 159 years in 1982 for poisoning 16 children at hospitals where she worked. There were remarkable similarities between Jones and Allitt, who undoubtedly was considered a copy-cat killer. Both satisfied an obsessive craving for attention by injecting children in their care with lethal drug doses. Both were dumpy overweight women who fretted about their health. Detectives didn't know whether Allitt read the book for sure, but it opened an intriguing line of inquiry. On police bail, Allitt was given refuge by her best friend, fellow nurse Tracey Jobson. Tracey, 24, took Allitt into her family home in Peterborough: an act of kindness that triggered a bizarre chain of events.

Bleach was poured on carpets, the bathroom curtains were scorched and a knife was found stuck in a pillow. Allitt calmly insisted that it was the work of a poltergeist. But Tracey soon realized that Allitt was the culprit. Allitt was severely deluded, however, when she wrote to her grandmother after being found guilty and told her that she believed that some of her former nursing colleagues were jealous of her intelligence.

The next news to hit the headlines in 1993 in the Allitt case was that the parents had launched a legal battle for multi-million-pound damages over the nurse's attacks. They said there was a crucial 17 days before police were called to the hospital and that evidence of Allitt's mental instability had been ignored. They also condemned the announcement by the Health Secretary, Virginia Bottomley, that an independent inquiry was to be held in private. The parents understandably wanted a full public inquiry. A lab report, 17 days before police were called, showed that

Paul Crampton had received the second highest dose of insulin ever recorded. If something had happened sooner, the parents argued, then one murder and three further attacks might have been prevented. The official inquiry was to be headed by Sir Cecil Clothier, the ex-NHS ombudsman. Irrespective of the legal action, parents were to receive immediate compensation. The Trent region denied the inquiry would be a whitewash.

Right to the end Allitt played for sympathy – "still the star of her own pathetic show" wrote the *Mirror*. But detectives believed her anorexia nervosa was self-induced – another symptom of her desperation for attention. Starving herself was the "trump card" in the killer's crazy fantasy, but she also used other tricks to stay in the spotlight. On remand, she suffered several mysterious injuries. At first they were explained away as accidents in the jail gymnasium, but it was harder to explain cuts found on her wrists … except as self-mutilation to seek attention. Her lawyers denied she had tried to commit suicide, and she even tried to win over prison officers; consequently, duty rotas were constantly changed so that warders didn't spend too much time with her.

Other victims that survived Allitt's heinous attacks included Patrick Elstone, whose heart stopped. He left Ward Four permanently damaged. Chris Peasgood stopped breathing but fought back from the brink of death, while Henry Chan, who also survived, turned dark blue and collapsed with a heart attack.

The papers then turned their attention to the relationship that the killer had with council worker Steve Biggs, who fell madly in love with Allitt. The bullying nurse would often fly into uncontrollable rages with Biggs, regularly punching and kicking him for no reason. He became a sex-starved target of her ugly violence. Steve became convinced that the girl he planned to marry was a lesbian in reality and said: "She loved to think she was always in control and manipulating things." The couple first met at the village pub in Corby Glen and, after a short romance, she proposed to him. However, she also tried, unsuccessfully, to seduce Tracey Jobson. Allitt surely lived in a world of make-believe. Biggs put up with the former nurse's bizarre behaviour for two years before he finally realized that she got a "kick" out of making him miserable. Allitt even claimed when their lovemaking failed that she had been raped by a previous boyfriend, but friends stated that too was made-up lies. It was another attempt to grab attention, they said. Allitt should perhaps also be held responsible for another death at the hospital, that of a night sister who killed herself with an overdose during the police probe. Sister Jean Saville, who was cleared of all involvement in the Allitt murders, took her own life due to the shock and horror of the children's deaths. Another nursing colleague explained at the time that all staff had been under suspicion and many of them felt guilty that the children had died. Although no other members of staff were found guilty of any crimes whatsoever, one said at the time: "Although there is no guilt attached to us now, we will never feel completely exonerated. There will always be that question lurking: could I have done more?"

Perhaps surprisingly, Allitt's family stood by her, and in 1993 it was reported that the killer nurse regularly cuddled a tiny tot in her arms while inside Rampton top-security prison. The baby in question was her sister's eight-month-old daughter, Katie. Allitt's father, Richard, still refused to believe that his daughter was capable of harming a baby and said: "We are convinced she is innocent. We don't think she has it in her to do the things it is said she has done." He spoke a week before the deranged woman was due for sentencing in late May that year. The whole family were said to visit the murderer regularly. Richard Allitt just could not believe that the girl who as a teenager used to earn pocket money for babysitting was a cold-blooded serial killer.

Not long after, two doctors at the centre of the murder horror were sacked by hospital bosses. They claimed that they had been made scapegoats for the tragedies and immediately launched a legal battle backed by the British Medical Association. Consultants Nelson Porter and Charith Nanayakkara were to be made redundant. Both were paediatricians on Ward Four but were told there were no longer posts following a reorganization of child care services. An internal inquiry after Allitt's arrest decided there had been communication problems between the doctors. Instead, four part-time consultants would be held responsible for child care, under the control of the Queen's Medical Centre in Nottingham. Both men applied for the new posts, but both were unsuccessful in their applications. Meanwhile, Prime Minister John Major ignored the demands of the parents of Allitt's victims and dug his heels in over the secret inquiry into the Ward Four tragedy. He refused calls for a public probe, despite massive pressure in the Commons, which sparked a storm of protest over his hardline tactics. MPs felt that Trent Regional health authority should face the witness box and should not be left with some control over the official inquiry. Labour leader John Smith slammed the "appalling negligence" involved in the case. But Major was adamant that a probe behind closed doors was most likely to get to the truth.

The papers continued their story of Allitt in 1993 with a report that she had struck up an "amazing" jail friendship with "black widow" Noeleen Hendley. She was also reported to have had at least two gay affairs since she had been incarcerated at Rampton. Allitt apparently fell for lifer Hendley, who had had her husband bludgeoned to death. The women became so close that worried staff had them moved to separate parts of the secure prison. They met in Newhall prison where Allitt then began writing of her bizarre life behind bars to a gay friend. In one letter she mentions a woman named Sharon, described as a "firebug", serving three life sentences.

Hendley hired a hit man to kill her husband because, as a Catholic, she could not divorce him. She was eventually trapped, largely by a revealing picture of a rose and butterfly tattoo on her thigh. Her son found it at the home of her lover, Terry McIntosh, and told police. Hendley and McIntosh were "consumed by a terrible passion" and had sex as often as possible, Nottingham Crown Court was told. They offered up to £5,500 to have Tony Hendley murdered. His skull was smashed by 29 blows from a rolling pin.

The deadly couple and the hit man were jailed for life in 1992 for murder. In the meantime, Sir Cecil Clothier snubbed angry parents' pleas for a public inquiry into the Allitt case, telling them in effect that "he knew best". He warned them and health workers that they would not be able to insist on giving evidence in public.

Allitt, for her part, had believed that she would be cleared of all the charges against her. However, she stood motionless in the dock on 28th May 1993 as the judge jailed her for life 13 times. It was thought to be the highest number of life sentences handed out in a British court in the 20th century. The judge also told the killer that "there was no real chance she would ever be freed". Allitt was taken to Holloway prison to begin her sentences. Her lawyers, however, claimed that she wouldn't live long if she wasn't transferred to a secure hospital. During her time in Rampton she had poured boiling custard on her hands and put glass in her mouth. She refused to eat and drink. She stood motionless as the judge branded her a woman without remorse. He also called her a serious danger to the public but urged "human containment" because she suffered from a severe personality disorder. Throughout the two-hour hearing Allitt sat with her eyes fixed in front of her, flanked by nurses and a doctor from Rampton. Not once did she look at the judge or the parents of her victims. It was the first time her skeletal figure had been seen in court since she was taken ill on the 16th day of the 51-day trial. Psychiatric experts told the court there was little hope she would ever be cured – and she still remained cunning and manipulative. Writing at the end of September 1993, journalist

Anne Diamond had this to say: "The Angel of Death tested her wings this week and found she could still fly. When I heard that Beverley Allitt was to feature in a TV documentary the other night, I feared the worst. That we would be glorifying a convicted murderer – chasing a grisly sort of celebrity, attaching a value to the words of a wicked woman. It was apparently, a chance meeting between herself and the Central TV crew who were in Rampton filming others. The reporter, quick off the mark, grabbed a word with her. This is where I start to feel uneasy. Very uneasy indeed. Because I stop reacting like a journalist – and start sympathizing with the parents [she] so cruelly robbed of their children. What the hell was he doing asking her if she admitted or denied the crimes? Is her guilt still open to question? I thought she'd been tried, convicted and denounced as the most wicked female serial killer this country has ever known. I recall the details of how her young victims screamed in their torture, after lethal injections brutally administered by this monster in nurse's costume.

"I remember the anguish of parents whose babies had died or been severely brain-damaged by her barbarism. It is a degradation of their tragedy to give her any sort of platform to air her views." Allitt was transferred back to Rampton after her behaviour at Holloway became intolerable. Diamond continued: "But while I cringe at the thought of Beverley Allitt enjoying a sort of fame, I must defend the right of the cameras to be there to record the facts. Because now we know how we treat our criminals. For the murder and maiming of innocent children, she leads an easy life.

She has her own room. She has assessment twice a week, goes to the gym, and can attend Saturday night dances. She listens to her Walkman for long periods and enjoys sitting quietly embroidering. The object of her toil? A child's cushion cover. As if that weren't enough to make your anger reach boiling point, she does it again. After the release to the press of a still-frame picture from the video footage, Beverley Allitt decides she does not want the TV report to be broadcast after all. She withdraws her consent, Rampton apply to the High Court and stop the programme going out. If attention is what nourishes sick Beverley Allitt, then she must be thriving right now, content in the knowledge that there's no shortage of willing pawns."

However, there were others who believed that Allitt was fooling the authorities so that she could remain in hospital rather than in prison. Dr David Enoch said she was a psychopath who would remain a psychopath and should be in jail. Meanwhile, the official report on the tragedy failed to single out any particular person responsible when it was published on 11th February 1994. The following day the parents of the victims slammed health authority managers in the press. They called for "heads to roll" among management and renewed their demand for a public inquiry into the murders. They were angry that doctors and nurses had lost their jobs, but not one senior official had been disciplined. Mrs Creswyn Peasgood said: "We have always believed there would be a cover-up and I have not changed my mind. Why have the managers who have been criticised in the report not been fired as well?"

Alan Davidson commented: "I cannot understand how someone with a severe personality disorder came to get a job as a nurse. She had a highly visible history of doing herself physical harm. I am not satisfied with this report. A public inquiry will give us the opportunity to cross-examine witnesses." Peter Phillips added: "I would have expected people in authority to resign. They should not be in positions of responsibility." Bob Quick of the health workers' union, Unison, said: "Blame is still being directed at junior staff and being deflected away from more senior levels." Ann Alexander, the lawyer representing a number of the victims' parents, slammed the report by Sir Cecil Clothier as "wholly unsatisfactory". She said: "It fails to address the main issues for which it was ordered. It will give no confidence to parents that any future crisis will be dealt with properly." Health Secretary Bottomley was accused of fudging the issue by saying that doctors, nurses and hospital managers were "collectively" responsible for not acting on tiny clues which emerged during the killing spree. But she insisted the main conclusion of the investigation was that a "determined and secret criminal" could defeat the best-regulated organizations. "The tragic events in Grantham were the product of a malevolent and deranged criminal mind," she stated, and told MPs "everything must be seen in that light". But Labour's Shadow Health Secretary David Blunkett said the need for well-staffed children's wards was the real lesson of the tragedy. In his report, Clothier had also highlighted inadequate staffing levels on Ward Four, but claimed that this would not have stopped Allitt.

The two doctors criticized in the damning report spoke of the devastating effect it had had on their lives. Both also hit back, saying the report failed to take into account problems posed by extreme staff shortages on the ward. Dr Charith Nanayakkara said: "It has destroyed me and my family. My reputation is at stake and my future uncertain. I have already publicly stated that if blame is to be attached to those who were unable to think the unthinkable then I may be fairly criticised. Even at the stage when police were called I could not believe that criminal activity was the cause of the collapses on the ward." Dr Nelson Porter said the inquiry was wrong to place blame on individuals: "We were working in such circumstances that the clinical demands of caring for our patients consumed our qualities of leadership and drive. These demands were compounded by lack of staffing and resources." Both doctors appealed after being made redundant when the management of the hospital was reorganized.

The report pointed to a series of failures which left the hospital vulnerable, including ineffective action by the ward manager when told of suspicions of foul play, and inadequate procedures relating to Allitt. There was a lack of meetings with staff from all disciplines and poor operational procedures and indecision by senior hospital management. The report also stated what needed to be done to avoid any future tragedies, which included checking the sick records of nursing applicants, reviewing the paediatric pathologist's role if a child's death was unexpected or clinically unaccountable, and asking for sick records from past employers. It also stated that applicants with an excessive use of counselling, self-harming behaviour or sick leave, should be free from professional help and in work for two years before being considered a suitable candidate, and that under no circumstances should anyone be employed if there was evidence of a personality disorder.

In July 1995, it was reported that a schoolboy who watched Allitt murder a baby while on Ward Four was suing hospital bosses for damages. Paul Lilley was 11 when the nurse attacked Claire Peck, just feet from his bed. He lay watching in terror as doctors and nurses tried desperately to save the small girl's life. For a while he could stare right into the dead baby's open eyes and finally saw her taken away in a plastic coffin. But throughout the drama, not one member of staff thought to shield him from the scene. Since that time he had suffered nightmares, speech problems and difficulties at school. His dad, David, said the happy and outgoing boy had became withdrawn, anxious and lacking in interest: "I feel angry and bitter. For years our lives have been ruined by Paul's ordeal." He continued: "It was a traumatic experience and it need not have happened." Lawyers issued a writ against South Lincolnshire health authority, claiming Paul suffered severe post-traumatic stress because of negligence. Just over a year later, in November 1996, parents were to share in £500,000 in compensation for post-traumatic stress. Twelve families were believed to be entitled to the payout. But, in July 1999, the family of Becky Phillips were awarded more than £2 million to help pay for Katie Phillips' care. The payout came after an eight-year legal campaign by the little girl's parents against the health authority. Mrs Phillips said: "I'm delighted that Katie's financial future is secure. The whole affair has taken a heavy toll on the family. Now we can move on." But, she added: "I'm still angry that Allitt was allowed to continue what she was doing without being detected." Katie has been left epileptic, partially paralysed and partially blind by evil Allitt. Mr and Mrs Phillips separated due to the stress they endured at the hands of Allitt. She hadn't just taken away the health of their two daughters, resulting in the murder of one and appalling harm to the other, she had also wrecked their marriage. The health authority was also told they must pay the costs incurred by the family in bringing the case to court. Just a few months later, Allitt was back in the news when the *Mirror* reported that "some of Britain's most dangerous criminals are enjoying a lavish fun-filled two weeks of holiday festivities at the taxpayers' expense". The article concentrated on Rampton Hospital's "extravagant" entertainment for 450 inmates, which included special menus for Christmas, games with cash prizes, karaoke, hired entertainment, quizzes, and free non-alcoholic wine and beer. The *Mirror* had been leaked details of the "Christmas and Millennium Programme 2000", which cost hundreds of pounds. One hospital worker slammed it as "sickening pandering". The newspaper obtained evidence that Allitt chatted and joked with her "pals" at the parties. They included the then 32-year-old's "boyfriend", Mark "vampire" Heggie, who drank the blood of one of his victims. Another hospital employee said: "It makes a mockery of justice." However, a spokesperson for the hospital said: "It is ridiculous to complain about what we are doing. It is sensible to keep patients occupied."

In July 2000, Allitt was guarded round the clock after a two-hour operation for self-inflicted injuries. She was taken to hospital to have surgery to remove items from her body. An insider said: "She had to be operated on under general anaesthetic. They found half a ballpoint pen, two paper clips and a metal staple inside her, so she was watched closely to make sure she couldn't do it again." She apparently felt that she had done her time. She was reported as saying: "I've done my time for killing those children. It's time I got out." Four staff escorted her in a secure van to Bassetlaw General Hospital for the operation. When she returned later that day she had a row with a fellow female patient who told her: "It's a pity you didn't die on the operating table." The insider said: "She has cut her wrists and arms before. She is clearly very disturbed. Allitt is pretty well confined to her room. Staff are making sure they know exactly where she is in case she tries to injure herself again. She must be in sight and sound of staff at all times."

Five years later it was reported that Allitt received £150 a month in state handouts. Up to the end of May 2005 she received £25,000, which, if this continued, would mean she was paid more than the £49,166 compensation paid out to the families of her victims. Understandably, the families did not react well to the news. It was slammed as criminal that someone who had killed should be allowed to save for her future. At the time, Allitt was also earning at least £40 a week for doing light duties in the kitchen or garden. Yet her crimes were so appalling that she was placed on the Home Office list of prisoners who should never be released.

In December 2007, Allitt failed to have her sentence cut. Mr Justice Stanley Burnton told the High Court there was an "element of sadism". He said the children's ward was turned into "something close to" a "killing field". Sue Laccohee, mother of Becky and Katie, said: "We will campaign vigorously to keep her under lock and key to her dying day."

Rosemary "Rose" West
(with Fred West)

1994

Towards the end of April 1994, police began digging at a second "Gloucester house of horror", the former home of builder Fred West and his missing daughter Charmaine. They planned to search a bricked-up cellar and a rear extension looking for more "grisly secrets" in one of Britain's biggest ever murder hunts. In a dramatic development, on 25th April West's second wife, Rosemary "Rose" West, was charged with murdering missing teenager Lynda Gough, one of the nine women whose remains were found at 25 Cromwell Street, Gloucester, in March 1994.

The *Mirror* published pictures showing the scene of the new search at 25 Midland Road, Gloucester, less than half a mile from the by then infamous address in Cromwell Street. Charmaine had lived at the house with Rose and Fred West in the early 1970s. She vanished about the same time as her mother, West's first wife, Catherine Costello. Officers planned to pull down a false wall over the only entrance to the cellar and demolish two bricked-up fireplaces in the reception rooms downstairs. They were also planning to search an area which was covered by a kitchen and bathroom extension that West helped build. A coal bunker was demolished to make way for the extension. Two circular rust-coloured stains on the lino under the wooden kitchen table marked the spot where police were told they should dig. The bathroom was expected to be ripped out in the search for clues to Charmaine's disappearance at the age of eight almost 20 years before. In 1976, four years after moving to Cromwell Street, West landed a job helping to build the extension at his old home. One former workmate, who asked not to be named, said: "He worked very hard as part of the team at the house. We all thought he was a nice guy." A former lodger at Midland Road said: "It is terrifying to think I could have been living on top of a grave. We always thought it was odd so many places were bricked up and nobody could explain why." The detectives leading the search installed a temporary office at the rear of the Midland Road house and the six male students who lived in bedsits in the converted house had been found alternative accommodation.

Rather than a random sweep, police were concentrating on specific areas of the dwelling, and, if necessary, planned to use a ground-penetrating radar to locate objects hidden under the floor. Detective Superintendent John Bennett, who headed the inquiry, said: "We will be searching part of the garden and one specific area on the ground floor near to where the extension meets the house at the rear. This will be an extremely difficult operation as large amounts of concrete, hard core and ballast were used to build the extension foundations." He continued: "It is possible that what we are looking for could have been removed when builders were excavating the footings prior to building the extension. We have no indication at present as to how long this search will take." Meanwhile, contractors were bricking up windows and sealing entrances at 25 Cromwell Street where digging was expected to finish.

Rose West appeared before Gloucester magistrates charged with murdering 19-year-old Lynda Gough. The 40-year-old was accused of the murder jointly with her 52-year-old husband, who faced a total of 10 murder charges including that of his first wife and his 16-year-old daughter, Heather. Lynda was two weeks away from her 20th birthday when she disappeared in April 1973. She had been working as a seamstress at a Gloucester Co-op store and had moved out of her parents' home to live in a city-centre flat. Rose West was also accused of two separate charges of raping an 11-year-old girl and assaulting an eight-year-old boy in the early 1970s. Bespectacled West did not speak during the brief hearing, and was then remanded in custody. Fred West was due to appear in court in May 1994.

Rose West was accused on 16th May of carrying out a sixth murder with her husband. Police in Gloucester said she had been charged with killing Juanita Mott, 18, who vanished in 1975. Later in May 1994, the *Mirror* published a photo of Heather West as she balanced on the climbing frame in the family garden. Four years later she was dead, secretly buried in the ground, just a few feet away from where she posed for the photo. Murdered Heather was hidden next to the remains of two other girls. Their bodies had already been there when she played happily on the frame with her brothers and sisters years earlier. On 27th May, her mother, Rose, was jointly charged with her murder. Rose and her husband were at this stage jointly accused of killing nine young women at their Cromwell Street address. Fred West was also accused of killing Catherine and eight-year-old Charmaine. Heather was just 12 years old as she dangled from the frame, but, in 1987, she suddenly vanished. Days earlier she had bumped into an uncle in the street, and the excited 16-year-old told him she had just got a job at a holiday camp. However, she never made it to her new workplace. She simply disappeared – and no one reported her missing. Then, in February 1994, police found her remains under a patio at the house in Gloucester. Buried close to her were Alison Chambers, 17, and pregnant lodger, Shirley Anne Robinson, 18. Nearby were the remains of Alison's baby, which died three weeks before she was due to give birth. By this time, police had found the remains of West's first wife buried in a field near his childhood home in the village of Much Marcle, near Hereford. The bones of their daughter, Charmaine, were discovered in the search at 25 Midland Road. Rose West was also charged, with two men, of raping two girls and assaulting a boy, causing him actual bodily harm.

On 1st January 1995, Fred West hanged himself in his prison cell. He cheated justice on 12 murder charges, but in a chilling confession from behind bars he confessed to murdering many more – the terrible toll was suspected to be as high as 60. Tearful and depressed after his months behind bars, West broke down and blurted out the full horror of his "sickening crimes". He told friends: "I have been a naughty boy and done some terrible things. I will be going away for a while. Sell the house and look after mum." Police believed West's toll made him Britain's worst serial killer. But he took many of his macabre secrets to the grave. In private meetings with his son, West said he had carried out many more murders than the 12 with which he was charged, and only he knew where the bodies were buried. After one court appearance, he turned to a warder and said smugly: "They don't know the half of it." His victims were all women and children. He died before he and Rose West were due to face a pre-trial hearing in February 1995. Officers at Birmingham's Winson Green jail found West's body at 12.55pm and a doctor declared him dead at 1.22pm. There was no suicide note from the killer who could barely write his name. It was almost a year since the Wests' home had begun to yield its dark secrets. Week after week the shocked nation watched as the victims were unearthed. Nine were found in Cromwell Street, one at Midland Road and two more in fields on the Gloucestershire border. Some of the killer's chilling boasts were made to his 21-year-old son, Steve. In an exclusive *Mirror* interview, Steve said: "Dad was very depressed. He was always in tears. When I first saw him months ago in the police station he said he had done it. Since then he has told me there were more and he has told me where." West was distressed when his wife turned against him. "He said he loved and missed her," said Steve. In the months prior to his death, West said he had taken victims from Cromwell Street to a remote farmhouse where he cut up the bodies. He said he could make more noise there than he could at home. "He has described the farmhouse with an old barn that has been shut for years," continued Steve. "Nobody knows where it is apart from me." West told his son that he brought some of the remains back to Cromwell Street in large asbestos water tanks. Steve tested his father's confession and to his horror found the farmhouse exactly as he had described. Police had told West, who confessed to three murders early on in the investigation, that unless he confessed to the rest they would pull down his house in a detailed search. He then told them of the other nine. A police source said: "West had killed so many people over so many years that he couldn't remember where they all were. He walked around his basement saying he had put one there, and one over there. Then he would change his mind. You could tell he had simply lost count." Meanwhile, Steve West had promised his father that he wouldn't tell the police about the farmhouse, so the *Mirror* informed them of his comments.

Police and Home Office inquiries were launched after West hung himself with a piece of twisted cloth torn from a shirt. He was a known suicide risk and officers were ordered to check on him at least every 15 minutes. A major probe was undertaken to determine whether that happened on the day he committed suicide, when the prison was running with reduced staffing levels due to the festive season. West Midlands Police appointed Detective Superintendent Mick Williams, based at Walsall Road police station, to lead the inquiry. A police spokesman said: "Det

Supt Williams will be compiling a full report for the coroner. At this stage there are no suspicious circumstances." It was felt that the death of a "high-profile" prisoner would renew pressure on the beleaguered Home Secretary, Michael Howard, and prison service agency chief, Derek Lewis, who were still reeling from criticism over the Whitemoor jail allegations. The then Shadow Home Secretary, Jack Straw, said: "Taken with the ever growing number of security lapses in the prison service, this is further confirmation that Michael Howard's grip on the prison service is far too weak. The public, and above all, the victims' relatives, had a right to expect that West would be kept securely until his trial."

The "house of horrors" murder investigation was sparked by a child abuse case against Fred West in 1992. Police officer Hazel Savage noticed during the case, which collapsed, that Heather had not been seen for almost seven years. Checks showed she had not claimed benefit or used her National Insurance number since 1987 – which at the time was almost impossible unless someone was made homeless, had a change of identity or was dead. Police were also informed of a "sick" family joke that Heather was buried under the patio. In February 1994, police obtained a warrant to search the back garden at 25 Cromwell Street and both Fred and Rose West were arrested on suspicion of murdering Heather, Shirley Anne and, at that time, an unnamed young woman. Heather's was the first body to be found.

Rose West was released on police bail, while Fred appeared in court and was charged with the murder of Heather. Police then found the next two bodies. In March, police began a house search and the fourth, fifth and sixth bodies were found in the basement. Bodies seven, eight and nine were discovered in the cellar and bathroom areas. In April the 10th body was found in Letterbox field in Kempley, and digging began at Fingerpost field, in the same area. That same month, Rose was rearrested and charged jointly with her husband for the murders of Linda, as well as Carol Cooper and Lucy Partington. She made her first court appearance as police began their search of Midland Road. In May, the 11th body was found, and by the end of the month Rose West had been charged with the murder of her oldest child, Heather, as well as five other killings. In June 1994, the 12th body and a foetus were found at Fingerpost field in Kempley, and both Fred and Rose found themselves back in court. The following month, Fred was charged with the murder of Anne McFall and an inquest formally identified the remains of three of the young women.

One young woman told how she cheated death at the hands of Fred West after he brutally raped her. The "sex-crazed monster" punched Caroline Raine senseless and took her back to 25 Cromwell Street. He trussed her to a bed and subjected her to a terrifying 12-hour ordeal before she escaped. Former beauty queen Caroline said of his death: "I hope the bastard rots in hell." Caroline was just 17 years old when West kidnapped her in his van as she went to meet her boyfriend. She woke to find herself bound hand and foot on a double bed in the cellar that was to become the grave of many of the Wests' victims. His "monkey-like" face leered down from above. The "evil beast" gagged her with masking tape and cotton wool, then raped and sexually abused her. Caroline recalled: "I was petrified. He said he would keep me in the cellar and he and his friends would use me for sex. He said when they'd finished with me they'd kill me and bury me under the paving stones of Gloucester." With a sinister grin, West told her there were a few women there already. Caroline was convinced she was going to die. Only when West was satisfied by his vile attack did she get her chance to trick him into undoing her bonds. Caroline's heart missed a beat as he drew out a knife and used it to brutally cut the tape from her face. She conned him into thinking that she would not run away. Then, when he dropped his guard, she slipped out of the house and fled. West was arrested and later convicted of indecent assault and causing bodily harm. He was fined just £50 before walking free from court. The chairman of the bench said: "We do not think that sending you to prison will do you any good." Caroline told the *Mirror*: "It made me feel like I wasn't worth anything. It had been a difficult decision to go to the police in the first place."

As the nation reeled in shock from the crimes of probably the country's most notorious serial killer, it was suspected that he was responsible for the death of missing teenager Mary Bastholm. Meanwhile, criminal psychologist Dr Paul Britton compiled a psychological profile of West and his wife, Rose. He worked out that West had been killing ever since his twenties and that he had become used to it. A police source said: "He said the only time that West didn't kill was when he was prevented from getting at people, because he was in prison or something like that. If he killed two victims a year, we worked out that the true total could be as many as 60. But West was a psychopath who kept his secrets locked inside his head. Now nobody will ever know the full extent of his crimes." Police believed that the murderer trawled the streets of Gloucester looking for likely victims. The smooth-talking killer had the perfect cover – his house was used by legitimate lodgers. The terraced home was known as "the cheapest digs in town". For a few pounds a night, the homeless could find a bed. But for some it also became their final resting place. Some of his bus stop victims were believed to have been tortured and sexually abused before being killed said newspapers at the time. Some of the bodies were hideously mutilated. The unborn baby of one victim was found buried in the back garden in a different spot from its mother. West, described by a member of his own family as a "complete nymphomaniac", even used videos to film his kinky encounters. He also made a cat-o'-nine-tails to punish some of his victims during sex sessions. His children lived in fear of him and were never allowed in certain parts of the house. That was where the "entertaining" was carried out. The tools found in his workshop were used to butcher some of his victims. Police took away a number of saws and hammers. Meanwhile, the *Mirror* reported that West did confess to killing Mary Bastholm near the village of Bishop's Cleeve in Gloucestershire.

The first of the 12 known murder victims was 18-year-old Anne

McFall – she had been born in Glasgow, where West lived with his first wife. She met West there and moved to the Gloucester area in 1966, living at caravan sites. She was last seen in April 1967, when heavily pregnant. She was a nursery nurse who looked after West's children. Her remains – the last to be discovered – were found in the Fingerpost field in June 1994 after a 56-day dig by police. West's first wife, Catherine, was thought at the time to be the second victim, although it was later proved that she died when she called at Fred and Rose's home looking for her daughter. Catherine had two daughters with West, Charmaine and Anne Marie. Charmaine, just eight, died in 1972. Her remains were found when the Midland Road search broke through the concrete kitchen floor. Lynda Gough's remains – the first murder which Rose was jointly accused of committing – were found below the ground-floor bathroom at Cromwell Street. Police found the remains of Carol Ann Cooper in the basement at the same address. The 15-year-old had been living at a children's home in Worcester. She was last seen on 10th November 1973, getting on a local bus after an outing with friends. Student Lucy Partington, 21, was in the third year of an English degree at Exeter University when she vanished in 1973. She had been visiting friends at Pittville, Cheltenham, and left around 10.10pm for the bus journey to her family home in Gretton, near Winchcombe. Her remains were also found in the basement. Another student, Therese Siegenthaler, 21, disappeared in April 1974. Her journey from her student flat in London to Ireland, via North Wales, was never completed. She too, was found in the basement. The eighth victim, 15-year-old Shirley Hubbard, had a new job at Debenhams, having just left school. She left work in Worcester on 5th November 1974 to travel home to Droitwich. Shirley never made it – her remains were also found in the basement of Cromwell Street. Juanita Mott, 18, told her pals: "I'm just popping out." She was never seen again. She left her home in Newent to travel to Gloucester 10 miles away. Her remains were found in the basement. Shirley Anne Robinson, from Melton Mowbray in Leicestershire, became a lodger at the Wests' house. Her remains, and those of her unborn child, were discovered in the narrow rear garden. She disappeared in 1978. Alison Chambers, 16, was born in Hanover, Germany, where her father was serving in the army. She settled with her mother in Swansea, South Wales. In 1979, she moved to Gloucester to work, under the youth training scheme, with a firm of solicitors. Her remains were the second to be uncovered in the garden. Heather West's skull was discovered by police under the patio of the Cromwell Street house on 24th February 1994.

Rose West was told of her husband's suicide by her lawyer in her prison cell – where she awaited trial for nine murders. She was said to be devastated by his death, even though she had turned against him since their arrests. Her solicitor, Geo Goatley, travelled to Pucklechurch remand centre, near Bristol, to break the news to the killer. He had to leave his own wedding anniversary celebrations to make the journey after hearing the news from journalists. He revealed later that Rose was seeking comfort from a nun who visited her in prison, and was "coping" with her husband's death. The solicitor added: "I told her to dwell on the positive things in her life and not the negative ones. I also told her that if the Crown case was flimsy beforehand, it is flimsier now. I have never represented Mr West and it is not for me to make comments at this stage. But, his death will clearly have implications for my client. There will be a lot of issues to be studied and discussed." The Wests had last appeared together in the wood-panelled and glass-fronted dock of Gloucester Court on 13th December 1994, when the magistrates fixed the date for the committal hearing. Several prison officers stood between the couple during the brief hearing. They were due to appear again on 6th February but, obviously, Rose West would now stand trial alone. It became clear following Fred's suicide that Rose, who had always vehemently denied the charges, would try to have the case against her dismissed.

She was known as Rosemary Letts – and was aged just 15 – when she first met West. They met at Bishop's Cleeve, near Cheltenham racecourse. Rose's parents were so upset that she was involved with an older man (West was her senior by 12 years) that they had her taken into care until she was 16 years old. However, by that time, Rose was pregnant and she moved in with West and his two daughters at a local caravan site. On 17th October 1970, Heather was born in Gloucester. On 29th January 1972, the couple married.

As the case began to unfold, a simple trapdoor was reported in the papers, because it hid many of the gruesome secrets of the Cromwell Street address that had been dubbed the "house of horror". Beneath the trapdoor was a staircase leading to the cellar. Neighbours had paid little attention when men dressed in overalls and wellington boots first started digging at the house, because they thought they were fixing a burst pipe or clearing a blocked drain. But slowly and surely the horror began to emerge. Two days after police arrived they found Heather's skull, buried five feet beneath the patio, which covered most of the 60-foot back garden. To begin with, Steve West had expressed his outrage at the police excavations. "It's ridiculous, it's unreal," he insisted. "She just left home when she was 16 – as any 16-year-old can – and I haven't seen her since." Police then discovered the other remains – bodies were found dismembered and laid out in neat rows.

Two days after Fred committed suicide, the *Mirror* reported that Rose West could net "up to £10 million from her story of life with her monster husband". Estimates of the possible huge payout came as West's lawyer battled to have the nine murder charges against her dropped. Goatley declared: "I always felt the case was flimsy against Rose and now it is even flimsier. I would hope the Crown will drop it." One public relations expert said: "If Rose decides to sell her story, she could walk out of prison to a fortune. She could make anything from £5 million to £10 million in three years."

The female killer stared blankly at the walls of her prison cell as news of her husband's death sank in, according to newspaper reports. It meant that the case against her could have collapsed.

There were no tears, no words of sorrow. "All the hate is gone," she said. "There's no one left to hate now." The *Mirror* said that Rose had grown to "bitterly resent" her husband for what she saw as his ultimate betrayal – trapping her in the Gloucester "House of Horror sensation" that had grabbed headlines around the world. Mother-of-eight West still denied any involvement in the murders. Experts thought that the charges should be dropped. West could make up to £2 million with a "best-selling" book and around £8 million in film and video rights. Fred reportedly told police that his wife had nothing to do with the murders. By this time, it was known that she had actually heard the news about the suicide through a phone call from the Home Office rather than via her solicitor who immediately drove to see her. Rose was then counselled by elderly Catholic nun Sister Mary Paul, from the convent of Our Lady of the Missions near Bristol. Rose had decided: "Fred was a split personality and there was a dark side to him she didn't know," said her solicitor. After Fred's suicide, she was kept under a special watch in case she tried to harm herself. It was up to the Crown Prosecution Service to decide if the case should be dropped, but Labour MP Gerry Bermingham warned them to take "very great care" over the Rose West case. For her part, according to Rose, all she wanted was to be with her children and grandchildren. Apparently, she didn't want any of her late husband's estate. "She is not materialistic," said Goatley. In other news, the mother of Alison Chambers revealed that she could not afford a decent burial for her murdered daughter. "I'm beside myself with worry that I'm not going to be able to give her a proper send-off after all these years," said a heartbroken Joan Owen. She also reacted bitterly to West's prospects of riches and said: "There must be something very wrong in this world if money can be made out of other people's suffering. We have been told we may be eligible for compensation. We don't know how much. But until we get the death certificate, we will not get a penny."

The next news to emerge was one of West's workmates telling how he unwittingly helped to lay the patio which hid three bodies. Horrified Robert Bashford said he carried the 2ft-square paving slabs into the back garden. "It haunts me to think what was underneath those slabs," he said. He told how he'd been working with West opposite the house two years prior when he was asked if he would carry in dozens of slabs to complete the red and grey chessboard-patterned patio. He also described how West gave him a tour of the house, during which the murderer "bragged about his handiwork and pointed out all the improvements he had made". Rob said: "We went into the main bedroom and he proudly showed me his four-poster bed with a mirror under the canopy. There was no doubt what went on in that room. Then he took me down to the cellar." Rob said that West talked of "frequent orgies". He added: "West told me he had hundreds of dirty videos and a video camera which he used to film women while they were making love."

Early in 1995, Glebe Farm, down a lonely lane in Bishop's Cleve, was identified as the farmhouse to which West took the bodies of victims in order to dismember them. Meanwhile, it emerged that

Anne Marie Davis, one of West's daughters, was suspected of trying to take her own life after hearing of her father's suicide. She was rushed to the Gloucester Royal Infirmary emergency department on New Year's Day, after it was thought she had taken a cocktail of pills and alcohol. The 30-year-old had her stomach pumped before being discharged. On 4th January 1995 it transpired that Rose West would stand trial for the murder of nine young women and girls. By 10th March, West had been committed to Winchester Crown Court for trial in the autumn, accused of 10 murders. On 6th October she stared impassively out of a steel box. She sat in the five foot by four foot cubicle, bolted to a prison van's floor. A woman warder was on guard outside. The newspapers called it the "Trial of the Century", as West was driven from her cell in Winchester jail to the Crown Court five minutes away. Two police officers accompanied the modified Peugeot jail van – at the time standard transport for all Category A prisoners – through sealed-off streets. Only a handful of bystanders saw West's arrival and departure. The trial began with the selection of the jury of eight men and four women. It was then taken up with legal arguments before the prosecution opened its case. West denied all charges. However, the court heard how the innocent victims of "murderous Rose West" died in agony, serving her depraved sexual appetite. Stripped, bound and gagged, they were subjected to "revolting acts of abuse". West and her husband picked which victims would die and which victims would live by deciding how likely they were to tell of their ordeal. Prosecutor Brian Leveson, QC, said: "Their last moments on earth were as objects of the sexual depravity of this woman and her husband." In a "blueprint for the horror that was to come," said Mr Leveson, vulnerable young girls were picked up by the Wests as they cruised the streets. He continued: "At the core of this is the relationship between Frederick and Rosemary West, what they knew about each other, what they did to others and how far they were prepared to go. In Rose West, Fred West had the perfect companion."

The couple had a ravenous appetite for depraved sex. Unwittingly, they revealed their "horror" to an innocent neighbour when they told that they would go out together looking for girls thumbing lifts. They would lure the youngsters into their car using the false security offered by Rose West. Then, they would persuade the girls to lodge with them at their home. They targeted, amongst others, girls who were running away, and those in care. Once in their clutches, the victims would be bound and gagged with brown parcel tape, cloth and rope, and abused in the "most depraved and appalling way," said Mr Leveson. One girl, Shirley Hubbard, just 15, was completely masked with tape from her chin to above eye level; she had a tube inserted inside her so she could breathe. She could not move. She could not see. It was not known how long she suffered like this "before the blessing of death came to her", the court heard. Alison Chambers was said to have had a belt buckled around her head to stop her from screaming. Rose West, it was said, got obvious pleasure from sexually assaulting a restrained and immobile girl with all the pain, humiliation and indignity she could muster. Mr Leveson said: "Those whom the Wests believed would not complain, perhaps because their involvement appeared to be willing or perhaps because of their vulnerability, lived. Those whom it was believed posed a threat, perhaps because of their injuries or perhaps because they may talk to the police ... death was the option for them." Those that died were then butchered. Eight of the nine bodies found at Cromwell Street in scenes "more terrible than words could express" had been decapitated. Most were missing a number of bones. Other had had their hips ripped from their sockets. The butchered bodies were then buried. Mr Leveson said: "Each was dumped without dignity or respect in a different small hole some three feet below the ground in the garden, the cellar and underneath a bathroom." Five of the bodies, the court heard, formed a grim circle of death, being buried in the cellar clockwise in the order in which they died. In court, it emerged that Caroline Owens had been picked up by Fred and Rosemary West. Another survivor, known in court as Miss A, told how she saw two naked girls. One was trussed up with packing tape. One of the girls was assaulted before Miss A was bound by tape by Rose West. She was then forced to have sexual intercourse with Fred West before she was brutally assaulted. She was just 15 years old at the time of the attack. Kathryn Halliday told the court how she had shared six weeks of sex with the Wests, during which time she was shown whips and hoods, and was blindfolded and tied to a bed. As the sex sessions became more and more violent, she left, pushed beyond her emotional and physical limits.

West remained composed as the story unfolded; however, when Mr Leveson described the "pathetic" remains of Heather – found with her head severed and the bones of her feet and hands missing – she dropped her head and wept. The air in court was "thick with tension" as the QC rose to his feet. West was flanked by two prison officers as she listened to the prosecution lawyer tell the jury to prepare for "horrific and harrowing" details. He began by saying the horror emerged after questions were asked in 1992 about the disappearance of Heather.

Forensic evidence proved that Heather's skull had been struck from her spine and her bones had been chopped up so that the remains could be forced down a small hole. When police found Charmaine's remains at 25 Midland Road, she too had missing bones. She had lain underneath the kitchen for nearly 23 years. Mr Leveson said that the Crown did not suggest that Rose West was responsible for the "field murders" of Catherine West and Anne McFall, but "she was responsible for the deaths of those named in the 10 counts". It was also not suggested that she acted alone, but that she and Fred West were "in it together". The QC told the court: "It was easier to get a young girl in the car while Rosemary West was in the vehicle, and they liked girls leaving home because the girls then had nowhere to live. In fact, on two weekends, Mrs Agius [the neighbour to whom they spoke of picking up young girls], babysat for them while they went off together looking for girls to pick up. Picking up girls in this way was one of the blueprints for the horror that was to follow." By this time it was widely known that Rose West "greatly disliked" her stepdaughter, Charmaine. In court, it was cited that the "hated" child was West's first murder victim. According to the prosecution, West "blanked out" at the mention of Charmaine's name "as though she never existed". Fred had lived with Charmaine, but was not her natural father. He also had Anne Marie from his first marriage by this time. After he met Rose, she was often left in charge of the two small girls while he was away. Shortly after West gave birth to Heather, Fred West was arrested for offences of dishonesty and remanded in custody. He was sentenced to 10 months in prison and released on 29th June 1971. Rose West was then 17 years old. While in the ground-floor flat with the girls West told a neighbour on a number of occasions that she could not cope with Charmaine. She disliked the child's rebellious nature and the fact that she could not curb and control the little girl as she wanted to. On one occasion, the neighbour sent her own young daughter to ask West for some milk. "Tracey saw Charmaine standing on a wooden chair with her hands tied behind her back with a belt. Mrs West had a large wooden spoon in her hand and she looked as though she was about to hit her." It really upset Tracey who told her mother, who then spoke to West about the incident. She was told that Charmaine had been very naughty and had had to be punished. By the end of the school term in July 1971, Charmaine was marked by the school as having left. After moving to Cinderford in the Forest of Dean, the neighbour, Shirley Giles, tried to see Charmaine, but got no further than the hallway of West's home. She was told that the child had returned to live with her mother. In fact, she had been murdered. Fred West was still in prison so West had to have murdered the child herself.

Years later, family friend Ann Knight became worried when she hadn't seen Heather for a few days. She asked West if the girl was ill, the prosecutor told the court. West said: "There was a hell of a row here a couple of nights ago. We found out that she was going with a lesbian from Wales and she had gone to Wales with her." Heather was the last to die and the first to be uncovered. "She would have been an infant, a toddler and a very young child when first Charmaine and then the others were killed one by one," said Mr Leveson. "There is no direct evidence that she knew what had been going on or what an examination of the cellar or garden would reveal. If she did know something, she would hardly be able to tell and certainly not while she lived at home. It is quite clear that there was growing friction between the Wests and their oldest daughter," he continued. "Heather does not appear to have had a boyfriend and this itself seemed to upset both parents. What is clear is that on or about June 16, 1987, four months short of her 17th birthday, she disappeared." Mr Leveson went on: "Ronald Harrison knew the Wests. He had a daughter the same age as Heather. He recalls that in September 1987 he asked after Heather, whom he had not seen for some time. He was told by Frederick West, in the presence of Rosemary West, that Heather had been assaulting the younger children whilst she was babysitting." The prosecutor stated: "The assaults had, said Mrs West, eventually resulted in her giving Heather a good hiding and a few days later Heather had left home. Both Frederick and Rosemary West told him she was fine and living in Brockworth, Gloucester." Mr Harrison then asked the Wests if they had been looking for their daughter, to which they replied that they had not. They explained that Heather would not tell them where she was living, but always telephoned to let them know that she was alright. It was simply untrue.

By the following year a number of people had heard West's explanations as to her daughter's whereabouts. She told the local window cleaner that her daughter had run away. Again, it was simply untrue. She told the man, Erwin Marshall, that they had informed the police. It was a lie. The prosecutor continued: "Heather didn't leave home. She was murdered and buried naked in the back garden. None of her possessions have been recovered, none of her clothes, none of her belongings, none of the impedimenta which an adolescent of 16 has by that age gathered around them – not a trace." He told the court that when Heather's dismembered body was found: "The bones were jumbled up. The only proper conclusion is that the dismembered body had been dumped in a random fashion. There were two lengths of rope, perhaps to tie hands and feet together. There was no gag." West was interviewed by police twice about her missing daughter, once in 1992 and then again in 1994. At the first interview she told police she had gone out shopping and come back to find Heather and all her things gone. In 1994, the story was told in a very different way: "Mrs West said that when Heather was almost 17, they had problems with her at school and that Heather had spoken about a job somewhere which had fallen through. She said that she had drawn £600 out for Heather, left it with Fred and then gone shopping." In the latter interview, before the body was discovered, she said she had been told by Fred that he had seen Heather in Birmingham and Bristol. Mr Leveson told the jury: "The precise motive for the death of Heather West is to a degree speculative. It could be because she knew too much about what had gone on and could not be allowed to leave home. It could be because there was a blazing row ... and Rosemary West did give her a hiding – and rather more than a hiding. It could be that Heather was resisting attempts to involve her sexually in the household." He added: "It is plain that you can and ought to conclude that Rosemary West participated in the killing of her own daughter."

The air was tense in court number three as the first horrific details of the case against Rose West were outlined. West was defended by barrister Richard Ferguson. In front of the judge, Mr Justice Mantell, was a doll's house-style model of 25 Cromwell Street. West sat at the back of the court, flanked by two women prison officers. Above West, but out of her line of vision, sat 52 members of the public, who had queued for hours to listen to the gruesome details laid before the jury. The 29 reporters and two authors furiously scribbled down the details as fast as they could, while an audio link was set up in two other courtrooms. Mr Leveson told the packed court of the horrific nature of the torture and murders carried out in the Gloucester house. Fragments of gags and makeshift bonds were found on the skeletons of the naked, dismembered bodies. What happened to Shirley Hubbard was particularly difficult for the court to hear. The plastic tube through which she breathed while kept captive as a "sex slave" was forced through the young girl's nostril. Two other pieces of tubing were also found by the dead girl. "The breathing tube or tubes demonstrate that Shirley must have been alive when the mask was applied. Its purpose can only have been to keep her wholly under control, unable to see, unable to cry out, just able to breathe. She had, you may think, absolutely no chance at all … she was kept alive but helpless; that can only have been for sexual gratification so that her living but restrained body could be used or abused at will."

The court then heard how Fred West had had an affair with 18-year-old Shirley Anne Robinson, who was pregnant at the time of her death. Rose West knew all about the affair. Fred West was the father of Shirley's baby. One lodger, Elizabeth Brewer, noticed increasing jealousy and annoyance from Rose West towards the younger woman, whom she had tolerated at first. Eventually, West told the DSS that Shirley had returned to Germany. This was yet another lie. It was stated in court that Fred West had become involved with 19-year-old Lynda Gough. Her mother knocked on the door after two weeks, and initially the Wests lied, saying that Lynda had never been at Cromwell Street. However, Mrs Gough noticed that Rose West was wearing her daughter's slippers and that some of her clothes were hung on the washing line. She was then told that Lynda had gone away. She alerted the police, the

DSS and the Salvation Army, but there was simply no trace of the teenager.

The prosecution's case continued. Alison Chambers had had her mouth and jaw firmly shut with a leather belt wound around her chin and up over her skull. Carol Ann Cooper was, like the others, found naked, which the prosecution said, along with the restraints used on her body, "point to the purpose of her abduction and the motivation for it". Serious-minded Lucy Partington had been decapitated. There were cuts to a number of her bones, and her hips had been forced from their sockets. Many of her bones were missing, particularly from the feet and hands. Again, there were no remains of clothes. Two pieces of cord were knotted around her jaw and there was tape and another piece of rope found beside the body. Mr Leveson said that Lucy could have been picked up by the Wests at a bus stop, and that the presence of Rose West "would have provided both reassurance and, if necessary, assistance to subdue an unwilling victim". Therese Siegenthaler had had her hips torn from their sockets too. She had also been decapitated. Professor Bernard Knight, the pathologist, confirmed that Juanita Mott had a severe fracture of the skull, possibly caused by a ball-headed hammer. The injury was probably inflicted after death. Again, many bones were missing.

After hearing what happened to the victims who didn't survive their ordeals, the jury heard what happened to 17-year-old Caroline Owens, who was initially hired by the Wests as a nanny. She was picked up by the couple while hitch-hiking from her boyfriend's home in Tewkesbury on 6th December 1972. Fred West offered to drive her to her parents' home in Cinderford. Rose West put her arm around Caroline and started talking of sexual matters, the court was told. She tried to kiss Caroline on the mouth and began to touch her hair and fondle her breasts. Fred West asked his wife: "What's her t**s like?", so Rose West then put her hand between Caroline's legs. Rose West continued to indecently assault the girl when Fred West stopped at a farm gate near a roundabout. Fred then punched Caroline in the face, knocking her senseless. When she came to, her hands were being secured behind her back with her own scarf and her mouth was taped. "The tape was wrapped round and round her face, over her mouth and ears and round the back of her head. Thus gagged, she was driven back to 25 Cromwell Street with Rosemary West holding her down and continuing the assault," said the prosecutor. "She was stripped naked by both Wests. She was laid on the bed, she struggled and her hands were once more tied up behind her back. She was then subjected to a series of sexual indignities. She was blindfolded, her legs held apart by Rosemary West whilst Frederick hit her with a leather belt. Mrs West performed oral sex. Mr West had intercourse with her," said Mr Leveson. The newspapers had reported that Fred West was fined for the attack, but in reality both husband and wife were fined. Rose West hadn't been on trial for the attack, but the details of this case were "highly relevant, because the circumstances in which it occurred – the background as well as the detail of what Mrs West did to Caroline Owens – go a long way to proving what happened to many of the unfortunate girls buried in Cromwell Street". Caroline's evidence would show that Rosemary West obtained sexual gratification from abusing and immobilizing girls and causing pain and humiliation. Mr Leveson told the court that the evidence of Miss A would also prove crucial in the case. He said that West made sexual advances to the then 15-year-old, but that Miss A resisted and left the property. However, she returned around six weeks later. "She had a long talk with Rosemary West and on that occasion recalls being taken into a room where there were two naked girls. She did not know either of them. She was then undressed by Mrs West. Mrs West removed all her own clothing. One of the naked girls on the bed was then secured with packing tape so that she was on her back and her legs spread apart. A vibrator was used on the girl by Mrs West. Frederick West removed his clothing. He had sexual intercourse with the girl. Rosemary West then turned her attention to Miss A. She was taken to the bed and she too was taped by Mrs West in such a way as to prevent her using her arms. She was turned faced down. Her legs were taped apart. Frederick West had sexual intercourse with her whilst Rosemary West fondled her thighs. She did not resist," said counsel. She was eventually freed by West and allowed to leave. The Wests obviously knew she would not go to the police. She didn't. She was ashamed and felt guilty. When the bodies were discovered, Miss A did go to the police. West's mother, Daisy Letts, became the first prosecution witness against her daughter. Clearly nervous, she almost broke down, and constantly fidgeted with a handkerchief. She only looked at her daughter once, but West stared at her mother intently as she gave evidence. She told the court how her daughter was just 15 when she first met 27-year-old West, the father of two young daughters, and how she and her husband hadn't taken to the "boastful" man. Mr Letts had his daughter taken into care in the hope of ending the relationship, but that only lasted until Rose was 16. The court then turned its attention to the riddle of the victims' lost bones. The disappearance of the bones suggested that some bodies were mutilated said the prosecutor. Most of the young women found had bones missing. Seven were without one or two kneecaps, some were missing neck, finger and foot bones. He argued that the bodies were buried soon after death, rather than moved to Cromwell Street as skeletons. One explanation for the missing bones was mutilation. Meanwhile, Mrs Letts had told the court that Charmaine was a lovely little girl, whom she didn't see after West told her that she had gone back to live with her mother in Scotland. Mrs Letts did not see a great deal of her daughter, son-in-law or grandchildren over a period of around 20 years. As far as she could remember, she had only visited 25 Midland Road a handful of times, and had gone to Cromwell Road around seven times. Her behaviour in court showed she was clearly a lady who had great respect for authority. She also explained that her husband's word was law, that she hadn't wanted to place Rose in care but felt she had had no choice but to obey Mr Letts' wishes. Tracey Hammonds, Charmaine's childhood friend, also gave evidence, as did Glenys Tyler, West's sister. The next witness was Caroline Owens, followed by former neighbour Elizabeth Agius, who told a hushed court: "Fred liked to listen, liked to watch. He wanted to know everything Rose did. Rose said if he wasn't there, she'd tell him exactly what happened." Mrs Agius meant that Fred West liked to watch his prostitute wife having sex with clients through a peephole in the wall of his home. She continued her testimony, saying that the Wests cruised the streets in their car looking for young virgins – preferably aged 15 to 17. Sometimes they would drive almost 100 miles to London. The girls were then offered a home and a chance of going "on the game". Mrs Agius had been asked to participate in three-in-a-bed sex, and to sleep with Fred West. She declined.

Fred West, she told the court, had talked of turning his cellar into a torture chamber. She didn't look at Rose West once during her evidence. But West stared at the woman in the witness box. On day seven of the trial, June Gough told the court how she went in search of her missing daughter, Lynda, and was told by West, wearing the girl's slippers, that she had left. In a moving account of her search for Lynda, June said that over the next 20 years she often walked past the house and looked at it. Once, "I noticed that the cellar doors had been bricked up and I shuddered. I don't know why I shuddered – I don't think I went past that house again." She said that the last time she saw her daughter was on 19th April 1973. "That is something that has always stayed in my mind and that is not likely to be something I will ever forget," she said.

It then transpired that Elizabeth Agius confessed to a detective that she did have a sex session with the Wests, the court was told. A statement she made to Detective Constable Gerard Watters was read to the court. Agius allegedly told the officer she became drowsy and blacked out after having a drink with the couple. When she came to, the statement said, she was in bed with the couple and all three were naked. The next day she still felt "strange" and "sick" and didn't know what the Wests had given her. She had been afraid to speak out because she was worried about her husband's reaction if he found out. When Liz Brewer took the witness box she told the court that the Wests obviously had an "open marriage". She told the court about Fred's affair with Shirley Robinson, and claimed that Rose had her own boyfriends. What the court didn't know at this time was that just a mile up the road from where Beatrice Pace had been accused of murdering her husband many years before, Rosemary West was known to have taken in "clients" in the back of her van in the Miners Inn car park in Sling, in the Forest of Dean. A number of lodgers, including Ben Stanniland, Alan Davies and David Evans, all told the court that they'd had sex with West. David Evans became a £3-a-week lodger at Cromwell Street when he was 23. Asked about his relationship with the accused, he said: "She was the landlady, but she came upstairs now and again because she liked sex."

On 13th October 1995, the secrets of "Rose's Room" were revealed in court. It was known as a "special room" and one lodger told how she used to turn up her radio so that she didn't have to listen to Rose's "excited sexual behaviour". The noises that Gillian Britt heard were not those of pleasure, but definitely those of a sexual nature. She found them quite disturbing and left the property after six months. Meanwhile, Miss A admitted in court that she had run away from home at the age of 14 with a man who turned out to be West's brother. She had had a brief relationship with Graham Letts in Cheltenham the year before she was assaulted at the Wests' home.

On 17th October 1995, a former lodger from 25 Cromwell Street told the court that she heard a girl screaming "Stop it daddy" from the cellar. Jayne Hamer and another visitor, who heard a girl screaming in the night for 20 minutes, were both giving evidence against West. The following day, Anne Marie Davis wept as she told the court that she was raped by her father and stepmother at the age of eight. She said that the attacks – which included being strapped to a U-shaped metal instrument – carried on until she ran away at the age of 15. On several occasions, her father had sex with her in the presence of his wife. Anne Marie told no one. "I was told I should be very grateful and was lucky I had such caring parents. I was led to believe that all loving parents acted the same." She repeatedly broke down as she gave the most harrowing evidence the court had heard. She described how her father and stepmother had taken her down to the cellar at the age of eight. "We entered the room and on the floor there were some cloths and tape. I was very frightened. I didn't know what was happening. I asked what these things were for. There was no answer. I then had my clothes removed. Rosemary did it. I was crying. I was asking 'What's going on?' … I was struggling. I had my legs crossed. I was screaming and crying. Because I was struggling so much I had my hands bound and was gagged. Rose was sitting across me. I remember this excruciating pain. I wished I was dead." Asked if Rose ever did anything other than restrain her, Anne Marie said: "She was laughing and smirking and joining in. She was saying to me it was for my own good, and to stop being silly." West then assaulted the child herself. It wasn't the only time that West sexually abused her stepdaughter. Anne Marie was also sexually abused by her father's and stepmother's "gentlemen" friends. She was given notes to excuse her from school games so that no one could see the bruising she suffered. A visit by one teacher who did call at the house after spotting bruising on the child resulted in Anne Marie receiving a vicious hiding. She also told the court that whereas she had always been a crybaby Charmaine refused to cry – which drove Rose West to distraction and greatly angered her. Anne Marie remembered Charmaine being tied to a bed once when she was little, but she didn't know why. After Anne Marie's evidence, the jury went to visit the crime scene at Cromwell Street.

All jurors were requested not to point to anything in the house, and not to talk while they were there. They spent 40 minutes in the semi-detached house. The judge asked them to tour the house two by two. Graves in the cellar and garden were marked with the names of the alleged victims.

West was found guilty of killing Heather, Charmaine and Shirley

Anne Robinson on 21st November 1995. West was given 10 life sentences at the close of the trial. Each sentence was the result of each and every conviction she received. Mr Justice Mantell told her: "If attention is paid to what I think, you will never be released." She joined Myra Hindley in Durham prison, bringing together two of the most evil women in British criminal history. West showed no emotion. Eventually, the "house of horror" was demolished out of respect for the victims that died at the hands of evil West and her monster of a husband. While the sexual abuse that West suffered at the hands of her own father may go a little way to explaining her depraved behaviour – and the fact that because of it she said: "My biggest problem was anger. The biggest problem I had was in relation to my father and Fred West" – it in no way excused the excruciating pain and terror she inflicted on her victims ... and no words of remorse for Anne Marie, which she eventually uttered, could ever "mask the granite in her heart".

Tracie Andrews

1996

Murder suspect, tearful Tracie Andrews, 27, pleaded for more witnesses to prove her innocence of the "road-rage" killing of her fiancé Lee Harvey. It was February 1997 and ex-model Tracie was flanked by legal advisers as she appeared in public for the first time since being bailed just before Christmas 1996. Lawyers said three new witnesses backed up her claim that Lee, 25, was stabbed up to 40 times in a frenzied attack by a stranger. The mother of one stared straight ahead with her arms folded while adviser Pat Alexander said she could say nothing for legal reasons. Tears welled up in Tracie's eyes when the Birmingham press conference heard she was staying away from Lee's funeral on 7th February because of requests from his family. Lee's mum, Maureen, later condemned the appeal. She said: "To do it two days before the funeral is bad. We've gone through enough." A social worker reported a road-rage incident just five miles from the murder scene near Tracie's home in Alvechurch, Worcestershire. The woman – nearly forced off the road – described a burly passenger similar to the man with staring eyes blamed by Tracie for Lee's murder. However, on 1st July 1997, it was claimed that Andrews killed her lover herself in a frenzied knife attack – then hid the blade in her snakeskin boot until she could get rid of it. She, meanwhile, had told police that Lee was stabbed to death by a passenger in a car that chased them down country lanes as they drove their Ford Escort home from a pub. However, prosecutor David Crigman told a jury: "There was no other car. There was not some mystery murdering motorist. It was her." He claimed that, after hiding the knife in her boot, Andrews threw it into a hospital toilet waste bin, which was emptied before police began to suspect her. But forensic tests showed a curved bloodstain in the top of her right boot which, Crigman told the jury, "may tell you something of the journey that the knife took from the scene of the murder". Mr Crigman said the couple, who lived together at Andrews' flat in Redditch, had a volatile and turbulent relationship. After a row, shortly before Lee died, they went for a drink at the Marlbrook pub, five or six miles from their home. Drinkers there noticed that they seemed ill at ease. The prosecutor went on: "It is the prosecution case that during that journey home their volatile relationship again exploded and a fierce and violent argument broke out. It would have started in the car. It led to the car being stopped and both of them getting out. When they were out of the car the defendant launched the most vicious attack on Lee Harvey." He alleged that Andrews rained more than 30 blows (it was actually 42) on her lover, mainly on his neck, face, back of the head, front of his chest, left shoulder and back. He said the weapon had been a penknife blade from an imitation Swiss Army knife and that: "The ferocity of the attack on the boyfriend and the area where the attack was concentrated, namely the neck, would quickly have rendered Lee Harvey defenceless." Both the victim's carotid artery and jugular vein were severed. He continued:

"It would have led to the immediate and massive spurting of blood pouring from his neck. No doubt he would have tried to move away from her but he could not have moved far before collapsing on the ground and dying." As the jury at Birmingham Crown Court was shown photographs of Lee's wounds, his mother burst into tears in the public gallery. "It is likely that the attack continued after he collapsed and abated only after her anger subsided," said Crigman. Lee was stabbed to death outside Keeper's Cottage in Coopers Hill, just a mile from Andrews' home. A witness, Richard Maine, who had been visiting Keeper's Cottage, left just after 10.45pm and heard a woman calling for help and an ambulance. Crigman said: "Was she tending the body of the man? No, she was not. Was she running to the house for help? No, she was not doing that either. She was standing by the driver's door with her back to the car and she was covered in blood." He said Andrews made no mention of Lee being stabbed by a pursuing motorist and Mr Maine did not hear another car speeding away. Mr Crigman told the jury that the evidence from the accounts of passing motorists Simon Baker and Elaine Carruthers would show there was no dispute between Lee and the driver of another vehicle on the night of the murder. All they saw was one vehicle travelling at a normal speed: "It was not involved in any moving motoring dispute with any other car." Mr Crigman said Andrews was taken to the Alexandra Hospital in Redditch where she made frequent visits to the toilet. He said that the toilet cubicle she used for long periods that night contained a waste bin which was emptied twice a day and the rubbish put

Women Killers

unchecked into the hospital's disposal system.

Meanwhile, the jury also heard that a little girl, who overheard the argument between Andrews and Lee, would give evidence via a video link. Stephanie Duncan, whose bedroom overlooked the murder scene outside the cottage, had been woken up by the sound of the argument. The little girl told police: "I don't think there were more than two people. They were shouting. They were arguing. It was definitely two people." The prosecution told the jury: "The Crown submits that Stephanie Duncan heard the row during which the murder occurred."

At the hospital, Tracie's orange top, imitation leather trousers and ankle-length boots were taken for forensic examination. Scientists later found a curved bloodstain in the top of the right boot, measuring two and five-eighths inches by one inch. The scientist would give evidence that the mark was made by an object, wet with blood, being inserted inside the boot. Andrews had suffered injuries to her left eye and was covered in blood, which was all over her hands, face and hair. "These injuries were caused by Lee Harvey in what was to be their final and fatal confrontation," said Crigman. He said Andrews told police her clothes were covered in blood because she had cuddled Lee as he lay dying. But the bloodstains were not consistent with the sort of smears made by cuddling. They were splashes of blood which occur when it is spurting from a victim onto the person carrying out the attack. It was also cited that often assailants repeatedly wielding a knife are cut. There was a tell-tale injury found on the outside of Andrews' right little finger, and police found four strands of her distinctive blonde hair clutched in the dead man's right hand. A clump of up to 100 of her hairs was also found stuck in a bloodstain on the left sleeve of her jacket. Mr Crigman continued: "When police questioned her about this she said her hair came out easily. This hank of hair," said the Crown, "had been hauled from her scalp, roots and all." Winding up his opening speech, Mr Crigman told the jury: "They had another of their rows, a fierce row. She stabbed him and he pulled a clump of her hair by the roots from the scalp. His blood was spurting on to her jumper and he quickly died. From that moment, she has firmly lied." Andrews, however, denied murder and the trial was expected to last three weeks.

For two and a half years Andrews and Lee had endured a stormy relationship. The couple met in 1993, and the following year the victim moved in with Andrews. Things were volatile and turbulent and Lee often packed up his things and moved back to his parents' – only to patch things up with Andrews and move back in. On three occasions, the couple's rows had led to police being called. On 1st December 1996, the day Lee died, the couple had argued "long and loud", before heading off for an evening drink. The woman who lived in the flat above them heard them arguing during the daytime. But Andrews stuck to her story that Lee was murdered during a road-rage attack. She said she was looking for a cassette when the bust-up started. "I told Lee to leave it," she said in a statement read to the court. However, she claimed that the scruffy Cavalier or Sierra then overtook them as Lee stopped and the two "drivers" got out. They shouted obscenities, she said, and then the other "man", who was fat, aimed blows at Lee's face. She went to comfort him, but the driver punched her and she fell to the floor. She said: "Lee was making a funny gurgling noise. I knelt in something wet. I put my coat over Lee, I did not know what to do."

In court, it was revealed that Andrews had bitten her lover in a nightclub just weeks before he died. A friend, Steven Girling, said that Andrews drew blood from Lee's neck during a row at the club, and Victoria Silcock, who worked behind the bar, said she saw the defendant punch Lee on the cheek. She also said that Lee had scratches on his cheek. In the Marlbrook on the night Lee died, regular Stewart Johnstone told the court that the couple sat silently at a table for about 15 minutes. There was no conversation – it looked as if both were sulking. Another witness, traffic police officer Ian Henderson, told the court that he'd had to separate the couple after a furious street row just weeks before the victim was stabbed. Yet another witness, neighbour Shirley Peters, told how she heard the pair swearing and shouting at each other up to three times a week. She said they had had an angry dispute lasting over an hour on the day Lee died, and even the hard-of-hearing mother of the woman who lived above the couple had heard them arguing.

The court then heard that Andrews could not answer six vital questions from a former police officer seconds after her lover was killed. However, she gave her and another person a full account minutes later. The allegation came from former detective Susan Duncan, who, with a friend, found bloodstained Andrews near

Lee's body moments after the frenzied attack. Despite Andrews' version of events, Mrs Duncan said: "I had my suspicions from the very beginning." Mrs Duncan, who lived at Keeper's Cottage, was one of the first on the scene, and used her former police training and her legal training (she was at this time a solicitor) to form questions to put to Andrews. Mrs Duncan thought it was vital that certain questions were asked, but Andrews couldn't answer any of them. Andrews knew nothing about the "men" that attacked her lover, nothing about the vehicle they drove. However, when the police arrived and questioned Andrews in Mrs Duncan's house, she clearly told them about a black Sierra and claimed that the man who attacked and killed Lee was the passenger of the other vehicle and not the driver. However, on 4th July, witnesses told the court that there was no other vehicle. Simon Baker and Elaine Carruthers, who were travelling in the opposite direction to Lee and Andrews, said they saw no other car for a distance of at least five miles. Meanwhile, a nurse told the court that Andrews used the toilet six times in three hours. As Andrews gave evidence in court, where she again denied the murder and insisted a strange man had attacked Lee, she was watched intently by the murdered man's parents in the public gallery. When questioned by Mr Crigman she denied she was lying. She rejected claims that she hid the murder weapon in her boot, denied she disposed of it at the hospital. It was her third day of giving evidence at her trial.

On 30th July 1997 Andrews was convicted of the murder of Lee Harvey and sentenced to life imprisonment. However, just moments before the jury announced its verdict she looked *Mirror* reporter Rod Chaytor in the eye and flatly denied she had had anything to do with the young man's death. As he interviewed her puffing on the last cigarette that she would smoke as a free woman for a long time, her pale blue eyes didn't flicker as she told Chaytor that what had been said about her in court was all lies. She even produced a love poem she'd written for Lee after she butchered him to death. Right to the end she stood by her story of a road-rage incident. It was only as she prepared to leave the court, having been sentenced, that, for the first time in 21 days, "the mask behind her perfect make-up slipped". It had taken the jury of nine women and three men five hours of deliberation to reach its unanimous guilty verdict. Andrews would appeal.

In 1999, Tracie Andrews finally admitted that she had killed Lee Harvey. However, Lee's mum, Maureen, was furious, claiming: "She is doing it to save her skin. She knows she's got to admit her crime before she can be considered for parole." Andrews, meanwhile, claimed it was Lee that first pulled the knife as they got out of the car on that fateful night in December 1996. She told of how she and Lee had fought violently until she was "seeing red", and then she "just went mad". It was reported in November 1999 that the killer would have to serve at least 14 years for her crime. The minimum sentence was imposed by the Home Office following her prison confession. Tracie served the last few months of her tariff at Askham Grange open prison in York. She was released on licence in 2011.

Andrea Yates

2001

On 27th June 2001, it was reported that the mum accused of drowning her five children was pregnant. Friends of Andrea Yates said they believed her baby was due at the end of the year. It could have led to a huge impact on whether prosecutors in Texas pressed for the death penalty. It wasn't clear at the time whether she, or her husband Russell, knew she was pregnant when she drowned Noah, seven, John, five, Paul, three, Luke, two, and six-month-old Mary in the bath just a week before. Yates, 36, had been treated for severe post-natal depression since the birth of Luke and had attempted suicide before she took the lives of her children. On the same day that the news was leaked of the pregnancy, Russell attended the funerals of his five small children. In an emotional press conference the week before he said he and his wife had agreed not to have any more children because of the depression. Meanwhile, Yates' lawyer, George Parnham, refused to confirm the pregnancy. However, he did say he was awaiting the results of blood tests carried out at the prison where Yates remained under 24-hour suicide surveillance. Mr Parnham said he had met psychiatrists treating the prisoner and stated: "My observation is that she is still in a very deep psychosis. We are having her treated and examined by very professional mental health experts." He said when the medication she was on took effect "there will be some ability to have a rational conversation with her". He added: "I've accumulated evidence in the last 24 hours that strongly suggests that her mental status will be the issue, which means entering a not guilty plea by reason of insanity."

On both sides of the Atlantic on 19th February 2002, two women, both accused of killing their children, appeared in the dock. In Britain, Angela Cannings, 38, was accused of killing her two baby sons. She was convicted, but the original conviction was overturned because they just didn't take place. She had been wrongly convicted and wrongly jailed for two crimes she did not commit. The convictions were overturned as "unsafe" by the Court of Appeal on 10th December 2003. However, the year before, like Yates, she stood in the dock accused of more than one murder. In the United States, Yates pleaded insanity.

The jury was faced with deciding whether the mother was "mad", or "just bad". It was a case that was to put the death sentence back on the political agenda in America. Yates pleaded not guilty by reason of insanity to capital murder when her trial began in Houston, Texas. Her lawyers said she was suffering from severe post-natal depression, did not get the right care and was taken off vital drugs two weeks prior to the murders. Prosecutors said she was sick – but sane enough to know she was doing wrong. If Yates was found not guilty she would be sent to a secure hospital, but if convicted she faced life in prison or death by lethal injection. The case triggered a national debate about how to deal with the sufferers of post-natal depression. Women's rights and mental health experts said she needed treatment not punishment.

When police arrived at Yates' home following her 911 call to the emergency services, they found seven-year-old Noah face down in the bath. John, Paul, Luke and Mary were found on the bed. Yates had also called her husband, Russell, at work to tell him she had "hurt all five of the kids and that she finally did it". Russell rushed home and was met by Sergeant David Svahn. Prosecutor Joe Owmby said: "She knew this was an illegal thing. It was a sin. She knew it was wrong." However, her defence said: "Post-natal depression with psychotic features is the cruellest form of mental illness. It takes the very nature of essence of motherhood – to love, nurture and protect – and changes the reality." He continued: "The psychosis and delusions ... were so severe that her ability to think in abstract terms, to give narrative responses – to connect the dots – was impaired." Russell blamed doctors and hospitals for her care: "I don't blame her a bit. If she'd received the treatment she deserved, the kids would be alive and Andrea well on her way to recovery." District attorney Chuck Rosenthal told interviewer Ed Bradley that the case cried out for the death penalty. More death penalties were carried out in Harris County, where the trial was held, than any other county in the whole of the United States.

Andrea's mother-in-law, Dora Yates, told the court that the woman was a "very gentle and loving person". She said she doubted that her daughter-in-law had known what she was doing when she killed the children. The jurors were shown 29 harrowing police photographs of the five children who drowned; after a heated battle in court between the prosecution and the defence, State District Judge Belinda Hill had ruled that the jury could see 29 of the 39 pictures. On 12th March 2002, Andrea Yates was branded a killer by the court. The jury took three hours and 43 minutes to dismiss her claim to have been insane during the killings. The jurors had been expected to be out for several days. Russell buried his head in his hands as the judge read out the verdict. The jury then had to decide if she should be executed. Yates' mother, Jutta Kennedy, pleaded for mercy for her daughter. The 73-year-old said: "I'm here pleading for her life. I've lost seven people in one year." The grieving grandmother had lost five grandchildren, her husband who died in the months leading up to the tragedy, and now her daughter. The state then abandoned its request for the death penalty after one of the expert psychiatric witnesses was found to have made a false testimony. Yates was sentenced to life imprisonment, but this was overturned on appeal, and in July 2006, a retrial jury found her not guilty by reason of insanity. She has remained in secure mental institutions in Texas ever since.

Janet Charlton

2002

A former escort girl butchered her wealthy lover with an axe during a kinky sex session, a court heard on 11th April 2002. Businessman Danny O'Brien, 41, was found naked, handcuffed, gagged and blindfolded, with an axe embedded in his head. Divorced Janet Charlton, 36, fearing he was about to dump her, had lured him to the bedroom then callously executed him, the jury was told. She draped her white fishnet stockings and a suspender belt over the axe and left a black leather bullwhip on the bed nearby. Prosecutors said Charlton struck 20 times. Blood and brain tissue were splattered on the floor, walls and ceiling of the bedroom. At first, the killer claimed she found her lover murdered after returning from the park with her four-year-old daughter, Amy. But, later, she told police that Mr O'Brien planned to sexually assault and kill her and Amy. However, Prosecutor Paul Worsley told Leeds Crown Court that Charlton was a "callous killer and consummate actress". Charlton then admitted to killing Mr O'Brien at his luxury country house at Midgley, near Wakefield, West Yorkshire, in May 2001, but denied murder.

Charlton, who worked under the name Natasha, met the businessman through an agency. She gave him £60,000 from the sale of her former marital home when she moved in with him. The money was to be repaid should the couple split up. The day before O'Brien died the couple had been heard having a row. Later, divorced O'Brien drove to Chatsworth House in Derbyshire where he made love to a former girlfriend in the grounds.

Mr Worsley described the scene that confronted paramedics called to the house after the alleged murder. He said: "In the bedroom, they found him naked, lying face down on the floor with severe head injuries and with an axe in his head. On his wrists were handcuffs, in his mouth, a rubber ball in the form of a gag, secured around his neck with a collar. He was wearing a blindfold and under his neck was a black stocking." The QC said Charlton hit her lover with the axe as he was kneeling. The court then heard how the murderer would have been covered in blood from "head to foot" as she rained down blows on O'Brien.

Charlton was cleared of murder on 27th May 2002, but she wept as she was jailed for five years for the manslaughter of Danny O'Brien. The court heard that she had launched the attack after months of "his sick sexual demands". She had denied manslaughter, claiming that she had acted in self-defence. She said that O'Brien had threatened to kill her and drag her young daughter into sex sessions. The six-week case had lifted the lid on a world of group sex, voyeurism, wife-swapping, bondage and violence. O'Brien, a bisexual who enjoyed watching animal pornography, had groomed Charlton into accepting an abusive relationship, the court was told. He was "extremely controlling, extremely obsessive and sexually abnormal" said a psychiatrist. But an ex-boyfriend claimed Charlton was also well accustomed to orgies before she met O'Brien. Former rugby league star Ian Thomas said Charlton had sex with 11 men in five days during a holiday in Spain. He met her soon after her divorce from husband Tony in 1999. Mr Thomas said: "She has always slept around. When we met, she turned to me in bed and told me, 'You do know that I'm going to have sex with other men don't you?' She was a real looker and knew she could pretty much have any guy." The relationship ended when Ian found her in bed with another man. He said: "It was inevitable. I adored her but she just used me for sex. Her sexual appetite was fierce. She wanted threesomes, foursomes, group orgies. You name it, Jan wanted it."

Charlton came up with the axe killing after watching a scene from the film *American Psycho*, said police. They found a video recording of the 30-second sequence from the movie among porn in the bedroom where the victim was killed. Killing him was "like swatting a fly", she had said. Afterwards she took her daughter Amy to a park before returning and feigning horror at the "discovery". She confessed to police six weeks later, claiming she could only remember the killing in flashbacks. The prosecution claimed that: "She has given the performance of her life." Sentencing Charlton, Judge Norman Jones, QC, said: "You have been acquitted of murder but convicted of manslaughter by reason of provocation and that is still a grave offence and it means you lost your self-control. You were imbued with the desire to kill or cause very serious bodily injury." The judge also said that O'Brien was a "flawed man with extremely depraved sexual proclivities". He added: "I am satisfied that he introduced you to some of these practices although to keep him happy you were quite happy to go along with them. Your own attitude to sex was relaxed if not promiscuous and you were more ready to indulge in these practices than others may have been."

The *Mirror* revealed that Tony Charlton had one of the most difficult jobs a father could face – explaining to his little daughter that her mother was going to prison for killing a man. Amy Charlton had admitted to her father, when asked, that she had seen her mother attack O'Brien. Charlton was haunted by what his daughter had seen. The lurid details that had come out in court of his ex-wife's sex life had convinced him that he didn't really know the mother of his child at all. While he came to terms with the unsavoury evidence, he could not forgive his ex-wife for subjecting their daughter to the ordeal. Amy had been worried by the "thumping sound" she could hear coming from upstairs while her mother was butchering O'Brien. It seemed that her shout of "Mummy" stopped Charlton from continuing to hit the man. Charlton asked Amy to keep what she had seen a secret, but the little girl didn't like secrets, Tony said. He had made the 50-mile round trip to collect Amy that afternoon and was slightly surprised that his daughter didn't want to go upstairs and say goodbye to Danny O'Brien. Now he understood why, yet Charlton acted as though nothing had happened and promptly took the child upstairs as if she were going to say goodbye to her mother's lover. He, of course, was already dead, and Amy knew that. The fact that Charlton behaved so normally and took her small daughter up the stairs to see the dead man under the pretext of saying goodbye, really got to Tony. "She just wanted to save her own skin by pretending she had no idea of the horrors that lay in that room. She claims Amy didn't see the body, but Amy has told me she saw red spots on the floor and Danny looking different. She said Mummy had told her Danny was poorly." Tony's priority was to give Amy back her childhood.

As well as avoiding a murder charge, Jan Charlton also won the fight not to pay for her defence. Appeal judges then shortened her five-year sentence to three and a half in 2003. They called the original sentence excessive. She returned home on 9th December 2003. She was picked up from Askham Grange jail, near York, by her parents, and driven to their home in Middleton, Manchester.